SCIENCE AND CULTURE SERIES
JOSEPH HUSSLEIN, S.J., PH.D., GENERAL EDITOR

MYSTIC IN MOTLEY

MYSTIC IN MOTLEY

THE LIFE OF ST. PHILIP NERI

By

THEODORE MAYNARD

Milwaukee
THE BRUCE PUBLISHING COMPANY

393

Nihil obstat: H. B. Ries, Censor Librorum
Imprimatur: ✠ Moyses E. Kiley, Archiepiscopus Milwaukiensis
Die 2 Februarii, 1945

To Philip Maynard

PREFACE BY THE GENERAL EDITOR

SHOULD the title of this book appear startling, the life of the saint described in it will prove no less so. To play the fool for the love of God was the delight of St. Philip Neri. Jesting was almost native to him, and a well-thumbed classic joke book, the product of an age-long Christian culture, was his *vade mecum* from the days of childhood. But it was his motive that supernaturalized the use of it.

When the strain of heavenly contemplation grew so intense within him that it threatened momently to snap the tenuous link between soul and body, the remembrance of a joke could bring him back to earth again. And when, at times, the love of God waxed so strong that his whole physical being throbbed with the violence of it, and his heart literally expanded until it permanently bent the ribs enclosing it, then again his last refuge was a merry jest.

Shakespeare's jesters, it has been held, are the sanest characters in his plays, but in the jesting of Philip there is a wisdom not of this earth. After all, God made laughter, and the use of it can be rightly motived and wisely supernaturalized, as Philip's laughter always was. It woke, might we not say, celestial merriment in heaven at the marriage feast of the Lamb.

Philip Neri was no Puritan! Yet, in spite of all his laughter, the Founder of the Oratory was a severe man — severe with himself, and sometimes with others who could profit by such severity, though in his soul there was always more than a parent's love for them. His physical life was supported by so slight a modicum of food that its continuance must almost seem incredible, and yet it stretched on to his eightieth year.

And let us be sure there was more than mere jesting in the life of St. Philip Neri. His days were full days, and few men have labored so persistently and so successfully, by night and by day, for the glory of God and the salvation of souls. If his contemplative life was an epic of prayer, his active life was no less an epic of labor for the spiritual welfare of men — and his work lives on today, not merely in the Congregation that he founded, but in the supreme accomplishments of men of genius who submitted themselves to his guidance, as did the humblest and most little of all God's flock. Philip's heart went out to all and his arms embraced them all, from the poorest laborer to princes of the Church who freely came to him.

Even in the early days, when his abode was an attic, and he sought out the Catacomb of San Sebastiano — its entrance hidden in the bushes — as a safe retreat for contemplation, his hermit life did not prevent him from going forth into the company of men in order to converse with them on the state of their soul. Though still a layman, he soon drew crowds to his preaching.

True, he was an incomprehensible saint, an impossible saint, and yet the most human of humans. Steadily, as we come more fully to realize this, our attraction grows, until we also fall beneath his spell.

He came early into contact with the newly founded So-

ciety of Jesus, and if there was one thing in the writings
of St. Ignatius that could particularly touch his heart it
must have been the saint's insistence on the desire to be
esteemed "useless and foolish for Christ's sake," who first
willed to be deemed so for us. Here, for Philip as for Ignatius, was the last steppingstone to the attainment of humility in its highest degree. Such, in brief, was the celestial
philosophy at the heart of this Mystic in Motley, as at the
heart of the soldier-saint of Loyola.

But in their tactics and methods, as this book makes
clear, a vast contrast existed between these two saints who
in different ways secured the same end, God's greater glory.

Finally, there was about Philip a peculiar charm that
powerfully attracted men to him. It was no mere personal
magnetism, nor was it the expression only of his holiness.
Rather it was a natural winsomeness of character that was
combined with a Pauline eagerness to be all things to all
men. In a word, it was an exquisite blending of grace and
nature. Few men have ever been so deeply beloved as was
this man.

It is true, we must take into account also the Italian temperament. He understood his people and they understood
him. But he spoke to their intellect no less than to their
heart; he swayed their will no less than their pliant emotions
and could mould it into iron firmness. Above all, the fire
of divine love that burned within him communicated itself
to those who in any way entered into contact with him.

With a simplicity of art suited to his subject, the author
has given us here an authentic, animated, and sympathetic
picture of the saint. He has utilized to advantage the authoritative sources at hand, and conveyed his findings in a
direct and telling way. He has relied on fact rather than

on emotion, and so has produced a vivid and faithful image
of the man loved on earth by his fellowmen and favored
from Heaven by a visit from Mary, the Mother of God.

JOSEPH HUSSLEIN, S.J., PH.D.
General Editor, Science and Culture Series

St. Louis University
June 20, 1944

CONTENTS

Chapter One

THE GOOD PHILIP

A BOY about nine years old was leaning out of an upper window in his father's house in Florence, saying a psalm with his younger sister Lisabetta. He was a singularly attractive boy, with a winning innocence of look. Everybody noted that he was most respectful, not only to his parents but to all persons older than himself. He was known in the city as *Pippo Buono* — the good little Philip. With everybody he was a favorite.

That he was saying a psalm with Lisabetta did not, however, indicate any precocious piety. Never was he known to put up little altars or to speak of becoming a priest or monk. In the rather barely furnished house there was a plaster statue of the Madonna and a painting of a virgin martyr in a little frame, and before these he usually said his prayers. But he also liked to say his prayers leaning out of the window, because from there he had the view of all the part of the city that lay on the right bank of the river. This was one of the advantages of living in the San Giorgio parish; he could see the campanile, and the Badia, and the towers of the Bargello and the Signoria, and, above all, the great dome of Brunelleschi. The good Pippo loved that view, and so he loved to pray overlooking the crowded quarters of men and under the open sky. And as he was fond of little Lisabetta,

1

he was teaching her to say the psalm with him, alternating the verses.

He had another sister, Caterina, who had been born two and a half years before he was and who, since the death of their mother in 1520, had assumed a kind of maternal officiousness.[1] This time, for some reason known only to herself, she tried to pull six-year-old Lisabetta from the window. Philip pushed Caterina away.

It may have been a harder push than he intended. That there was a push at all caused great surprise. For the boy had so sweet a temper that it was commonly said that he did not know how to be angry. Coming from him, the slight petulant gesture hurt more than it would from any other child. It hurt him even more than it hurt Caterina. Even in his old age he was still speaking with remorse of that trifling exhibition of irritability.

That the good Philip should have been so very good tempered was all the more remarkable when we consider that his father, although of an admirable character, was of a gloomy disposition, for he was disappointed and unsuccessful. Rather late in life he had taken up the profession of a notary, remembering perhaps that an ancestor of his during

---

[1] Few notes will be found in this book. But, as St. Philip Neri's biographers do not always agree on details of this sort, I point out that the Abbé Ponnelle has established certain dates. Caterina was born on January 25, 1513, and Elisabetta on February 7, 1518. Philip himself was born on July 21 (or 22), 1515 at 2:00 in the morning. Their mother had died on September 8, 1520, shortly after giving birth to a son who was baptized as Antonio and who died soon afterwards. Cardinal Capecelatro, without giving any dates for the birth of the sisters, says erroneously that they were both younger than Philip. He also believes that the stepmother of whom we hear was not that of the children but of their father. Here Ponnelle, the latest and most thorough investigator, accepts Bacci's statement that the father had in fact married again. In these pages the researches of Ponnelle and Bordet have been used to correct and supplement the still indispensable lives of Bacci and Capecelatro, but with regard to the mother-in-law, Capecelatro's statement would seem accurate.

the latter half of the fourteenth century had been in turn the factor for the Archbishop of Florence, the Signoria, and the Archbishop of Fiesole. But Philip's father had unfortunately forgotten that Florence swarmed with notaries, and so he made no headway in an overcrowded profession. Getting few clients, he took up alchemy and neglected what business he might have obtained. Yet on formal occasions he continued to wear the *lucco*, the long robes of a notary. Though the ones he had were of coarse material and were threadbare, they indicated at least a definite social position. With this he had to console himself as best he could.

There were other ways in which Francesco Neri tried to assert his gentility. He once presented his son with an elaborately drawn and possibly somewhat fabulous family tree. His brooding upon such things did not improve the family fortunes or his temper. He seems to have withdrawn more and more into himself and so became to his children slightly indistinct — a pious and upright man, but a bit frosty and out of touch with reality.

The charm that was to be the boy's lifelong characteristic must have been mainly derived from his dead mother, though more may have come from the morosely romantic Ser Francesco than is at all apparent. The household fortunately was in charge of his stepmother, Benedetta Lenzi-Corazzei, and her sister. As Benedetta — who may not have been much older than her son-in-law — was of an affectionate and cheerful temperament, she largely made up for the loss of the children's mother and of a father withdrawn into brooding when not engaged upon such scraps of legal business as he could secure.

It was lucky for all of them that they did not have to live entirely upon his profession of notary. From his father, Ser Francesco had inherited a little property at Castelfranco, and his wife, Lucrezia da Mosciano, had brought him another little property at Monteperstoli as well as a dowry of fifty gold florins. On this the family managed somehow, though when Francesco died in 1559 — Benedetta being by then dead, Caterina and Lisabetta married, and Philip already famous in Rome — the household goods consisted only of a few kitchen pots and pans, a copper watch, a bag for holding papers and books, a couple of wooden stools, a broken trough, some patched clothing, and a bed. In addition there were a couple of casks of wine, the only articles to which any value could be attached. They suggest that in his lonely old age, when even the philosopher's stone had eluded him, the disappointed notary may have solaced himself with Chianti. Though he was able to leave his little property intact to his children, his shrewd daughters, when their brother resigned his share of the tiny fortune in their favor, agreed to accept it only on condition that their father's debts did not exceed what the legacy might bring in.

He was a man everybody respected and he might also have been a lovable man had he been born under a different star. As it is, we see him as stiff and shadowy, and we hardly see his wife Lucrezia at all. Of her we know little that is definite except that she was the daughter of a carpenter but with some prentensions to noble blood — something common enough to the Florence of that time, in which a vague aristocracy existed side by side with a passionate and ineffectual democracy. By now the city was wholly dominated by the Medici — mere merchants who had become princes, splendid, tyrannical, but (even in the royal exaltation to which several members of the family attained) sometimes slightly streaked with vulgarity.

The boy Philip grew up during the struggle of Florence

against the Medici and saw the brief triumph of the commune over the tyrant. The spirit of Savonarola was still very much alive. Though the Medici Leo X was pope at the time Philip was born, and as such was hailed even by the city that hated his forebears, yet people remembered how, when his father, the Magnificent Lorenzo, lay dying, Savonarola had been summoned to shrive him. "You must repent," the friar told him; and Lorenzo said he repented. "You must give up your ill-gotten gains," he was then told, and even to this the dying man hesitatingly agreed. "And you must restore the liberties of Florence." At this Lorenzo turned his face to the wall and died unabsolved.

It was a terrible death that Savonarola himself was to die six years later, a death on the scaffold. But Florence continued to look upon him as a martyr. And many years later, Philip, by then himself acknowledged by everyone to be a saint, drew a nimbus round a portrait of the friar. He never spoke about politics, but he always venerated this flaming theocrat who had proclaimed Christ King of Florence.

Yet between Philip and Savonarola there seem to be few points of similarity, though possibly for this reason he felt all the more free to honor him as a saint without committing himself to the Florentine political dreams. The friar was, above all else, a reformer, and the reformer's role was the very last that Philip ever wished to play, even when the time came when he was pressed by his disciples to play it. He therefore took Savonarola as a hero, but not as a hero to be imitated. Not for him anything like that stormy career.

At San Marco, where Ser Francesco had friends, Philip also made friends among the Dominicans. It was his custom to say that all the good he ever acquired came from them. From some of the older men who had known Savonarola the boy must often have heard stories of him at which he was thrilled. But San Marco had other ghosts — among them those of St. Antoninus and Fra Angelico. In the lovely and luminous frescoes of the great painter — still so fresh from his brush — Philip could see the piety that had impelled the Blessed Angelico to paint them on his knees. It was this spirit that was really much closer to his own than the violence of Savonarola.

In spite of all this he never showed any wish to become a Dominican himself, though he was subsequently to be "adopted" by the Order in the sense of being given a share in its spiritual treasury and, after his death, the singular honor of having his office included in that of the Dominicans, just as though he were one of their own saints. Instead he listened as a boy to their preachers and duly shivered at the tale told by the friar Zanobi de' Medici of how, when going to his usual confessor, every one of his sins was swept aside with "Oh, that's nothing!" until he suddenly saw that it was the devil before him in his confessor's guise. On the guileless lad an astrologer[2] named Zoroaster, who had been at the Papal court, pronounced, "If he were only a religious, he would be perfect."

His perfection was to be of a different sort. Not yet had he reached any crisis in his life. As Capecelatro says, the spiritual beauty that others besides the astrologer discerned in him "was a splendor, not such as clothes the perfect saint, but such as befits a saintly child." His was the same sort of charm that he might have seen in a little girl, eight

---

[2] The terms "astrologer" and "astronomer" were likely to be used at times without any precise distinction. The man's presence at the papal court did not necessarily imply that he held any kind of official position, even for a short period. He could, however, have been patronized *as an astrologer* by some of the courtiers or foreign representatives without the pope's knowing anything about him. In the Process he is mentioned without further comment, seventy years later.

years younger than himself, whose gay and smiling face he could have often passed in those animated streets. It was that of Catherine de' Ricci. If he ever did notice her in Florence, she was the first of many canonized saints to be encountered by him.

There were others besides the Dominicans that he listened to entranced. In April, 1527, when the Constable of Bourbon invaded Tuscany, Fra Balduino, the famous preacher of the Umiliati, got the news while he was in the pulpit. Breaking off his sermon, he told the vast crowd to cry out with him, "*Viva Cristo!*" When they did so, he assured them, "Know, O Florence, that at this moment God hath delivered thee." And so it proved. The imperial army without entering Florence went on to the sack of Rome. Yet though the Medici were expelled and, after a great speech by Nicolò Capponi, Christ was again proclaimed King of Florence, and though the Dominican Benedetto da Foinano blessed and gave to the Gonfalonieri a banner on which was painted Christ's image, in the end, after a long struggle and an unavailing defence during the siege, Alessandro de' Medici came back in triumph in May, 1532. It is not impossible that this failure of popular liberties had something to do with the events that were about to happen to Philip Neri. Be that as it may, it is certain that he left Florence soon afterwards. To his sharing the Florentine love of France we may trace, at least in part, what he was to do in old age by way of securing the throne of France for Henry IV. It was the only political action he ever performed, and though it was assuredly due to something more than his Florentine prepossessions, it nevertheless showed that, sixty years after leaving his city, Philip Neri was still a son of Florence.

There were other things the highly impressionable boy

derived from the same source and which were always to
remain with him. The two most oddly assorted of these were
a book of poems and a book of jokes, the *laudi* of Jacopone
da Todi and the *Facezie* of Arlotto Mainardi. They are not
mentioned here merely because of the piquant contrast but
because Philip Neri is not to be truly seen without them.

Jacopone was not a Tuscan but an Umbrian writing for
the most part in his native dialect. Nowhere, however, were
his poems sung more than at Florence — at San Michele,
which had gone in for *laudi* for more than five hundred
years, and at all the monastic churches, including San
Marco. While it would be too much to say that they were
unheard of at Rome until Philip introduced them, it was he
who certainly gave them an immense vogue there. From this
joyous hymn-singing was to come, by the aid of Animuccia
and Palestrina, the musical form of the oratorio whose very
name indicates the place from which it originated. All this
went back to Florence where an eager boy shared its distinctive popular religious fervor, and where he, too, now
and then tried his hand at the making of verses.

But though the *laudi* of Jacopone da Todi were of course
much more important in the history of the world than
Mainardi's jokes, the jokes were probably even more important so far as Philip's personal story is concerned. Though
the *Facezie* did not make Philip a humorist — a humorist he
would have been in any event — we all know how a book,
especially one encountered at the right moment, can come
as a revelation to youth. To him the posthumously made
collection of jests and stories seemed then the most delight-
fully amusing thing he had ever encountered. Indeed, it
always seemed so to him. A time came when a habit of
ecstasy was to be so fastened upon him that the only way
he could bring himself sufficiently down to earth to say

Mass was by having a page or two of this book read to him first.

It contained the quintessence of the Florentine spirit, at any rate of one side of that spirit, which was a kind of eccentric *bonhomie*. And Piovano Arlotto, as he was generally called, had much to do with the formation of an unusual kind of saint. "Is it not a wonderful thing," asks the editor of the jovial abbate's book, "that this man, with his goodness and his keen sense of humor, should have caught the fancy of all men, and made brothers, friends of them?" In that question he, so to speak, prophetically depicted Philip himself.

There were, it goes without saying, vast differences between the make-up and manner of life of Mainardi and Neri. But both were "characters," and had Philip not decided to become a saint he might have been another Piovano Arlotto, who "went from place to place, accompanied by his innumerable friends, eating and drinking, and entertaining them with his pleasantries." Even that description would apply to Philip except for one phrase. Mainardi's eating and drinking did for a while scandalise St. Antoninus, as bishop, until, looking into the matter, he decided that it was all sufficiently harmless. But Philip, though he was to take enormous crowds — sometimes as many as two or three thousand at once — to picnics in the vineyards near Rome, gave them no more than an egg and a bit of bread and a cup of wine to wash down the light repast while musicians played and sang to his followers as they sat quietly on the grass. As for himself, he ate practically nothing at all — so little that he took what small quantities of food he consumed in private in order not to arouse comment on his austerity. Apart from this, he was always a kind of disciple of Mainardi. His life was to be so jocular as to cause the young

Goethe, when on his travels in Italy, to bubble in many enthusiastic pages about the humorous saint. It would be quite possible to compile another *Facezie* from the light-hearted jests of Philip Neri.

Yet we do not hear of many pranks played by Philip when he was a boy; those were to come later. A mischievous youngster, however innocent he may be, is sure to get into trouble with his elders. At this stage the title people gave him was not Merry Philip but Good Philip. The only escapade we do hear of did nobody any harm nor (as it fortunately turned out) harmed himself. That was when, at about the age of eight or nine, he jumped on a laden donkey, not noticing how near the animal was to a flight of steps. Down the stone flags they rolled together, and those who pulled the boy from under the donkey thought that he had been killed, as he well might have been. But that was something that might have happened to any boy of his age; there is nothing else of the kind to record.

This, however, may be because we know very little at all about Philip Neri's early years. We do not even know the house in which he lived. Though in 1838 Florence put up a marble tablet on the house in the Via Mazzetta at the corner of the Via del Gelsomino to say that it was there that the infant Philip was put out at nurse, nobody has been able to establish with any certainty the location of the Neri home. One conjecture puts its site in the Via Chiara; another says that it now forms part of the Convent of the Convertite.

On the other hand, we are better informed about Philip's schooling. It was not out of the ordinary, but he had for master a man named Clemente, who had something of a reputation as a Greek scholar. Philip himself learned no Greek from this or any other source, but he did become well

enough grounded in Latin to read the scholastic authors
with ease — a common accomplishment at the time. He followed nothing that corresponded to university studies, nor
did he show anything of the temperament of a bookish man.
If later, in Rome, he took some courses in philosophy and
theology, he never tried to make himself into a scholar.
Those who came to be surprised at the mastery a supposedly unlettered priest showed of St. Thomas, need not
have been surprised, after all. Philip had an extraordinary
agility of mind and a phenomenal memory. He picked up
lightly what dullards have to plough through doggedly.
For his purposes he managed to acquire all the education
he needed. In the case of one so clever as he was, it stretched
a very long way.

When his schooling ended we are not informed. Possibly
it was when he was sixteen. Louis Ponnelle conjectures that
he may have acted as his father's clerk during his last months
in Florence. But he thinks that the best positive argument
in favor of this — apart from its inherent likelihood — is still
weak. That argument is that there is a resemblance between
the handwriting of father and son. This might suggest that
the notary taught the boy to use the clerkly script he himself used when drawing up deeds and similar documents.

Whether or not such an argument is weak, Philip would
seem to have shown no inclination for treading in Ser
Francesco's footsteps. And the notary was only too well
aware from his personal experience that his was not a profession in which it was easy to make a decent living. Therefore when a cousin of his, living at San Germano between
Rome and Naples, offered to take the boy into his business,
holding out also the prospect that he might make him his
heir, the offer was accepted. At the end of 1532, or early
in 1533, Philip set out to find his fortune.

Chapter Two

THE FORTUNE THAT FADED

EVERYBODY knows that the Italians of Philip's time were famous all over Europe as bankers, and that Italian manufactures made many a commune rich. Yet reading of the life that people lived, one wonders when they did any work at all. The explanation must be that, while they applied themselves to business, they were too tinglingly alive to be entirely engrossed by it. Some such explanation certainly would have to be offered for Philip while he was at San Germano; the only things we hear of are the things that he did outside of business hours. Presumably he did spend some time at his desk; we get the impression that he had nothing to do. In his case the truth is that he had an all-important personal problem to settle. He was not idling, but he could have given little time to what he was supposed to be doing.

That he went to a place like San Germano — the present Cassino — might seem strange. For it is now an insignificant town with hardly any trade. In those days, however, it was an important point between Naples and Rome, and the harbor of Gaeta served it as well as the road between the two great cities. It was there that Romolo Neri had prospered in trade and had built up a fortune which, while not enormous, may have seemed so to the poverty-stricken Neris in Florence. With Uncle Romolo — he was Philip's uncle only by courtesy, being really Philip's second cousin — there was a wonderful chance for him to get on in the world. The disappointed Ser Francesco, bemused by the philosopher's stone, conjured up visions of boundless wealth in his romantic fancy.

To get there meant a journey of three hundred and fifty miles for Philip, which in all likelihood he made on foot, carrying with him nothing but a couple of shirts and perhaps a book or two. When later Lisabetta sent him two more shirts, he wrote to tell her that they had been ruined in transit and that she had better not send any more. That he did so was probably a sign that he was already meditating a course of action of which he knew his family would not approve, and that he did not want to put himself under even the smallest obligation. For when passing through Rome on his way to the South, he may well have felt, by those deep instincts by which he was always moved, that it was in Rome that he was to live his life. If so, he said nothing about it but went on to the Uncle Romolo who was expecting him.

What is certain is that he soon discovered that he did not want to remain with Uncle Romolo. Just how long he did remain is not at all clear. In later life Philip said that it was only a few days, something that Father Matthews, his recent Oratorian biographer, regards as a mere fashion of speaking, pointing out that Italians are notoriously vague about time. On the other hand, it would appear that the period of two years which has been suggested would have to be ruled out. Father Kerr would not seem to be far from the mark in commenting in a footnote to his translation of Ponnelle and Bordet: "There is no difficulty in reconciling a stay of several months with the various authorities." It is, in fact, hardly possible to believe that Philip was at San

Germano — or at any rate in the vicinity — for a shorter time than that before going on to Rome.[1]

We quite definitely know that Philip lost little time in telling Uncle Romolo that, much as he was obliged for all his kind offers, he was not going to accept them. He did not take long to see that the commercial life was not for him. But to decide just what his life was to be called for a period of meditation and prayer. This he had at the near-by monastery of Monte Cassino and at Gaeta. If any doubts have been cast upon his having been there, it is only because some people wish to take Philip's "a few days" quite literally and to send him on his way to Rome at once.

It is possible that the supposedly fabulous fortune of Uncle Romolo had never had any attraction for Philip; he may have gone to San Germano only in obedience to his father and intending to escape at the earliest opportunity. But it seems more likely that it was at San Germano that he encountered the crisis of his life and that this was a complete surprise to him. He could have gone there with the full intention of settling down to his clerkship — and then have found something altogether different. Even in a counting-house the finger of God can touch a soul.

As to Philip's visits to Monte Cassino and the possible new orientation they gave, we have, as the Abbé Ponnelle points out, only evidence of a later date. Nothing is said about any such visits in the Process of Beatification. To this, however, it might be answered simply that one would hardly expect to find witnesses on this point appearing nearly sixty-five years later, nor would their evidence have much

---

[1] Father Antrobus in his edition of Bacci accepts Gallonio's statement that Philip went to San Germano when he was sixteen. This is an effort to account for a stay of two years. Eighteen, however, remains generally accepted as Philip's age when he went there.

bearing on the questions then under consideration. Though Bacci, whose life of St. Philip appeared in 1622, is silent about Monte Cassino, he is definite about visits to the chapel at Gaeta, and this was in charge of the Cassinese Benedictines. Let us start there.

Near Gaeta there is a mountain that rises abruptly from the sea. It is split from top to bottom by three huge fissures, and these, according to tradition, were torn in the rock at the hour of Christ's death. There the Benedictines had built a church dedicated to the Trinity and, in the central fissure (the largest of the three), where a mass of rock had lodged itself two thirds of the way down, stood a chapel dedicated to the Holy Cross. Placed where it was, it seemed to be hanging in mid-air, a circular building only seven yards in diameter, reached by thirty-five iron bars fastened to the rock and leading from the church above. On it a Crucifix was painted, clearly visible from the sea. Sailors, passing it by day, saluted it by firing guns. At night, when they could not see the Crucifix, they could see a light shining over the water. Then they would cry, "It is the Trinità!" and bare their heads and pray as they rounded the cape into the harbor of Gaeta.

There is another tradition about the place, one to which Dante refers in his *Inferno*. Gaeta is supposed to be named after Caieta, the nurse of Aeneas, and there it was — according to one version of the story — that Circe had detained Ulysses for more than a year. But if Philip knew about this legend, it would surely have interested him much less than the one about the sundering of the rocky mountain at the hour of darkness. In any event, what would have appealed to him most was that in this chapel, so remote, and reached only with so much difficulty, he could find complete retirement, and that from its porch he could gaze over the sea and the Pontine Marshes and the range of the Apennines. All through his life he loved to pray where he had wide vistas and the sky visible overhead. "Here," Bacci writes, "Philip was in the habit of retiring for prayer and meditation on the Passion of his Lord. It was during these retirements that his disdain of earthly things grew on him little by little, and he deliberated on the best means of putting into execution the design which he had conceived ever since his coming to San Germano, of leaving trade, and giving himself up to God in a state of life in which he could serve Him with less hindrance." It was here that the turning-point in Philip's life was reached.

But now for Monte Cassino. It is scarcely conceivable that Philip, when he was so near the most famous monastery in Europe — one consecrated by the graves of Benedict and his sister Scholastica — would not have gone there. It is true that it was his custom to make most of his decisions not under human guidance but under what he believed to be the direct promptings of the Holy Ghost. Yet when, eighteen years later, he decided to become a priest, he did so only because of what amounted to a command from his confessor. And at this stage he was surely even more in need of advice. However clear his ideas may have been, he could hardly have dared to trust them without consulting those expert in the spiritual life. What more natural then that he should have gone to Monte Cassino to seek some direction or at least a confirmation of his own intuitions?

We do not have to rely merely on such conjectures. As it happens, there was a book published at Venice in 1641 written by a Benedictine in which we find the passage: "Philip laid the foundations of a pre-eminent sanctity at San Germano and in Monte Cassino, in which place for three continuous years he drank in the spirit of piety and of holy virtues, mainly under the guidance of one of the most religious monks of Monte Cassino, Eusebio d'Evoli, a patrician of Naples." That is very specific, even though it comes a little late, and though it is not at all easy to account for the "three continuous years." Nevertheless we cannot look upon Monte Cassino as playing anything comparable to the part that another Benedictine abbey, that of Montserrat, did in the life of St. Ignatius Loyola. Still less may the bird's-nest chapel of the Holy Cross be considered as Philip's Manresa. We may safely conjecture that there were consultations with Eusebio d'Evoli, and perhaps other monks; beyond that it is not safe to let conjecture go.

One thing, however, may be reasonably inferred. It is that when the great resolve was taken, it must have been reached, as Bacci says, "little by little." Impulsive as Philip's temperament was, not even he can be imagined as forming his design within a few days. And though it is hard to picture him spending his life in the making of money — as hard as to picture St. Francis of Assisi as a prosperous shop-keeper, asking brightly, "What is the next order, please?" — in neither case can the career be explained adequately on the ground of a distaste for counter and counting-house. Each man had a clear vision and followed it without hesitation. When they turned their backs on bourgeois respectability, it was to become saints.

In short, all that we know about Philip's conversion is that it occurred at this time. We can, however, be sure that conversion, in his case, did not involve any turning away from sins of special enormity. While it is true that Philip was given to telling people, even when he was recognised by all as a great saint, that there was no good in him and that he was the worst of men, he also let out facts which show that no life could have been more innocent than his.

He did not have even the kind of ambition — in most men to be regarded as laudable — that held Francis Xavier back so long from the Ignatian net. When he confided to young Francesco Bozio that "after his conversion, he wept for his sins," we can only conclude that these sins were magnified by the extreme delicacy of his conscience.

The Abbé Ponnelle suggests that the sin for which he wept tears was one of indecision — that he was torn between a worldly career and a life wholly devoted to religion. This may be true in a certain sense, though we must remember that Philip does not seem at any time to have been even faintly touched with worldliness. Moreover, this was not altogether because of supernatural grace; his constitution was that of the poet — he was, in fact, writing poetry — and material success would have had little natural appeal to him. Conversion with him was no more than a decision to yield himself once and for all completely to God. It was resolving to be something more than the good young man he already was; it was the choice of sanctity. There could have been no question of renouncing this or that particular thing; what was involved was the renunciation of everything.

This renunciation is what accounts for all that has to be related of Philip. It was of the most absolute kind, and therefore of the most difficult kind. But its very difficulty may well have filled his mind with the doubt and indecision for which he afterwards wept as sins. As Capecelatro puts it: "He did not turn away from wealth and ease to become a monk or a friar, though he knew and loved both the Dominicans of San Marco and the Benedictines of Monte Cassino; but he chose to be, if I may say so, even poorer and more forsaken than these. He did not enter into a family of men poor like himself, whose brotherly love stands instead of wealth; he proposed to remain alone, a layman, and in poverty." Never did he take any vow of poverty; there was no need for that. When, as it were in spite of himself, a religious institution formed itself around him many years later, never would he permit those who joined it to bind themselves to poverty by a vow. He had only to look about him to observe that the vow of poverty often means that while the individual member of a religious order owns nothing personally, as a member of a community he may, in fact, own a good deal. So Philip would not even become a mendicant, living on alms from the well-disposed. It was his principle to ask for nothing. And in days that were to come, when one pope after another was trying to persuade him to accept the cardinalate, he made a point of remaining personally unprovided for.

While pondering his great decision he could hardly have had much time to give to Uncle Romolo's business. The good man must have been bewildered by Philip's refusal of all the glittering prospects laid before him. It was in vain that he now put into explicit words what had always been at the back of his mind — that he would make Philip his heir. That made no difference, except perhaps to harden the resolve of renunciation.

Had Philip said that he intended to become a priest or a monk, Uncle Romolo would have had something he could have understood, something within ordinary experience. But Philip had no such intention: he could not explain what he meant to do, for he did not yet know just what it was. Merely to throw up everything and to go wandering away — that must have seemed madness to Uncle Romolo. As in duty bound, the honest merchant did his best to dissuade him, reminding Philip that he was the last representative of his family and that he should not do anything so rash as what appeared to be in his mind. But all arguments were useless. Philip thanked him for his kindness and assured him that it would never be forgotten, "but that as to the rest, he was more pleased with his affection than with his advice." To avoid the pressure that was sure to be brought upon him from home, he did not even tell his father what he proposed to do.

His stay at San Germano was not so brief that an unbroken tradition is unable to point out the very house in which he lived, or even the room he occupied in the house. But it was more likely six months than two years. Toward the end of 1533 he left. He had arrived with a couple of spare shirts; when he went away he took with him nothing but the clothes on his back. To San Germano he had come to seek his fortune; to Rome he would go to traffic in the merchandise of heaven. No wonder that Uncle Romolo could make nothing of it.

Ponnelle remarks that the young traveller may have passed on his journey northwards two other men of a very different stamp. Benvenuto Cellini had at that time got into one of his scrapes and was being looked for by the *sbirri*. On his way to Naples he met his friend Solesmeo da Settignano, the Tuscan sculptor, who was on his way to San Germano to do some work upon the tomb of Piero de' Medici at Monte Cassino; and the two artists "jogged on together" singing along the road. But the heyday of such people was about over. The sack of Rome had brought the flamboyant glories of the Renaissance to an end. Philip was about to enter a city still desolated by what had happened in 1527. It was also one in which the period of reform in the Church was about to begin.

Chapter Three

THE HERMIT OF THE STREETS

FROM the large plan of Rome, which Leonardo Bufalini drew on wood, and from the sketches made by Martin van Heemskerk and the descriptions left by Johann Fichard about this time, we can obtain a good idea of what the city looked like when Philip Neri entered it. Smaller than Paris and London, it lay mostly in the low-lying districts between the Tiber, the Pincio, and the Capitol, a jumble of crooked streets. Wide stretches within the circling walls were almost completely uninhabited. There, for the most part, stood only ancient ruins or great lonely churches and monasteries. The general effect, so far from being pleasing, was depressing. Rome, moreover, had still to recover from the effect of the sack.

Though the Counter-Reformation, as it is inaccurately called, had not yet got into its full stride, yet the reforming spirit in the Church — the true Reformation — antedates the Lutheran revolt and was not called into being by it. This was particularly true of Spain, even if in that country reform often manifested itself in an unlovely character, one moreover that mingled political ambition with religious zeal. But even in Rome itself, where the inertia of the Curia was a brake upon decisive action, signs of impending change appeared long before any strong official efforts to heal the ills of the Church. Indeed, the deferring there of those efforts was, at least in part, due to the consciousness of Catholicism of its own vitality. It could afford sloth. There was time for a little more sleep before anything needed to be done. Not till 1545 did the Council of Trent open its deliberations.

The sack of Rome, however, had brought a very rude awakening. It was not the spring of events, for these would have taken place — though probably a little later — even had the sack not occurred. Men had long seen that reform was inevitable. Ten years, in fact, before that catastrophe the Oratory of the Divine Love had been founded at Rome, and in it most Church historians discern what the Abbé Ponnelle calls "the first cradle of Catholic reform." It was small enough and purely voluntary, and though strict in its demands upon the individual members, changed its officers every six months. A mere society, it had no other end, it declared, "than to root and plant in our own hearts divine love, that is to say, charity." But by degrees it attracted to itself the most fervent hearts in Rome, all of them actuated by one thing — the desire for personal sanctification, a sanctification to be won by love of God.

This love proved its genuineness not simply by pious exercises but by corporal works of mercy. Only a few years later, indeed, two of its members, Gaetano de Thiene and Pietro Carafa (who as Paul IV attempted reform in a manner sometimes injudicious) founded the Theatines. But at this stage, the activities of the society were directed not so much to combatting heresy as to comforting human misery. The greatest of its external works was the founding of the famous Hospital of the Incurables. Work in the hospitals was during this whole period one of the most signal indications of Christian zeal.

Only by personal services to the sick, crowded together

and neglected in wards where they were allowed to die like flies, could any help be brought to them in those days. The horror of these institutions passes all description, passes our imagination. "I was sick and ye visited me," meant something very different then from what it does in our own time. Not only did such work cry out to be done, those who did it taught themselves to see in those whose suffering they were alleviating the person of Christ Himself. It was to Him that they offered their services; it was from Him that they received grace. In a little while we shall find Philip Neri playing his notable part in such institutions of charity. For in them was the normal, almost the inescapable outlet of piety. To such work rallied all those in whom burned the love of God. Inefficient as may have been the help they gave, if judged by modern medical standards, their methods were immensely efficient in promoting personal sanctification and, through that, the fervor necessary for the reformation of the Church.

For the moment, however, Philip sought to gain his spiritual bearings by living a life of complete retirement. His true vocation — one of intense activity — was developed by a long period of preparation, and his work was gradually forced upon him by the pressure of events and the guidance of God. Until then he was nothing but a hermit of the streets.

There were many such in Rome, some of them rather eccentric characters. Most prominent among them was Franz Titelmans, the Capuchin, who had resigned his professorial chair at Louvain to devote himself to the sick in the Incurabili and to preaching in the streets. These wandering preachers and prophets in fact created so much of a problem that the Council of the Lateran at the end of 1518 had tried to curb their unauthorized and (it must be admitted)

often ill-advised activities. But there was nothing much that
could be done. Such men, however eccentric, were usually
orthodox enough. One could not suppress them merely because they chose to go about in rags, exhorting bystanders
to flee the wrath to come and to do penance. If they starved
and scourged themselves and beat their breasts with stones
in public, the popular (and even the official) mind recalled
that similar things were recorded of some of the saints. The
worst that can be said of them is that their energies, being
diffused and undirected, accomplished nothing substantial.
That they made their strange protest was recognised to be
one of the signs of the times.

Philip, though he adopted their hermit's robe and hood,
did not adopt their extravagances. When later he did his
own preaching as a layman, it was in a very different
fashion. For the time being, he was living in seclusion, thinking only of God and of uniting himself to God. The period
of his lay apostolate did not begin until some years after
he had arrived at Rome. To one so humble, so obscure, and
so inoffensive, no exception could be taken. He went his
way alone and undisturbed.

On reaching the city he had gone immediately to the
custom-house in the Piazza Sant' Eustachio. It may be that
he carried a letter of introduction from Uncle Romolo to
the official in charge, a Florentine of the name of Galeotto
del Caccia. On the other hand (since no mention is made
of any letter), it is quite possible that he went to Caccia
merely because they both came from Florence. Whichever
way it was, Caccia at once took to his open-faced fellow-
countryman and told him that he might sleep in the attic
of his house near by. The arrangement was probably intended to be no more than a temporary one, until Philip

could settle himself somewhere permanently; but it continued until 1551, a period of over seventeen years.

At first the family wanted to supply Philip with his meals. He would accept nothing except a *rubbio* (about eight bushels) of corn a year and a handful of olives every day. The corn he handed over to a neighboring baker who undertook to supply him with a roll of bread daily. This he munched, with the olives for meat, washing the repast down with a cup of water drawn from the well. It was as a rule his sole meal. Often he ate nothing at all, sometimes going without food three days in succession.

His little room had a bed in it, but that was not always used. Many nights Philip stayed up praying or wandering in the Campagna. When he did sleep, it was as likely as not on the floor. He hung what few clothes he had on a cord stretched from wall to wall.

In return for this lodging Philip undertook to act as tutor to Caccia's two sons. One suspects that he was not obliged to do this, and he certainly gave a hundred times the value of what he received. But he did not wish to be beholden to any man, and in teaching the boys he could do some service to God as well as to the director of the custom-house. His pupils' mother and aunt were to testify many years later that under his charge they became like little angels. Both, at all events, became exemplary priests, Michele as rector of the church of San Donato at Citille near Florence, Ippolito as a Carthusian monk.

With these two boys Philip no doubt showed that gay gentleness that was so characteristic of him. Otherwise during this period he avoided all conversation and came and went like a ghost in silence. He was afterwards to talk a great deal and to be the most accessible man in all Rome, but these first two years were spent as a solitary. Even in the animated streets of the city, he was almost as much alone as was St. Ignatius in the cave of Manresa. His silence and seclusion would have been absolute had he not sometimes felt moved to give a little instruction in Christian doctrine to the bands of beggars who hung around the doors of the churches.

He sought, however, a still more complete withdrawal. A favorite devotion of his was making the visits to the Seven Churches — a devotion he was to popularise and on which, when he began his apostolate, he was to take with him huge crowds. It was different in the beginning; all by himself he would creep out, usually at night, and make the rounds. From St. Peter's he would go, across the Ponte Quattro Capi, to St. Paul's Outside the Walls, and then on to St. Sebastian's, St. John Lateran, Santa Croce, San Lorenzo, and Santa Maria Maggiore. It was a distance of about twelve miles, and as Philip made the journey, with long prayers at each basilica, it must have taken at least eight hours. "Those who saw him as he walked along," writes Capecelatro, "so humble and so poor, alone, and rapt in meditation, would hardly suspect the mystery of that pilgrimage, or the consuming love hidden within that heart." Yet he began to be spoken of, unobtrusive as he tried to be. Word of it even got back somehow to Florence, and one of his family there, hearing about it, said, "I do not wonder at it, for I remember very well what Philip was when he was a boy. When you return to Rome, ask him to pray for me."

Prayer — that was his whole life. He never found it difficult to impel himself to pray. Rather, he was obliged on occasion to do violence to himself to stop praying and to attend to his little affairs. Michele and Ippolito had to be taught. When he was free, he would sometimes spend as long as forty hours on end rapt in God.

A favorite place of prayer was the catacomb of San Sebastiano. It was at this time virtually the only one of the catacombs of which people knew, for the very existence of the others had been all but forgotten. Even the true character of these labyrinths was not generally understood until 1578. And among the first of the scholars who set about making a serious study of these Christian antiquities was Philip's own disciple, Baronius. Philip himself must have been, in those days, about as ignorant as everybody else, though he may well have perceived, in however dim a fashion, that in the catacombs he was close to the very heart of the early Church. But his catacomb, we must suppose, was to him mainly a place where he could be perfectly secure from intrusion. All he had to do was to pull aside the thick bushes that concealed the opening, and he was alone, with no fear of interruption.

Not often did he go there by day. In the moonlight he would walk along the Via Appia Antica, as then constructed, past the ruins of the Baths of Caracalla and the tomb of Cecilia Metella — the *Capo di Bove*, the people called it, as they still do, because of the heads of the oxen on the frieze. This being the case, he did not see much of the wall paintings in the labyrinths. It was not to see them that he went; he was concerned solely with prayer. The Dominican novice-master at the Minerva used to point him out in later days to his novices as "the man who had lived ten whole years in the caves of St. Sebastian's." The exaggeration was not so great that it need trouble us.

Perhaps in all this there was a romantic and even a slightly morbid taste. Certainly the expeditions had their terrifying

moments and inevitably induced, even in Philip's cheerful
spirit, a streak of unhealthy excitement. There is small wonder that he began to see diabolic apparitions. One day as
he was passing the Colosseum, the devil came to him naked,
trying to inflame his imagination with filthy thoughts. He
dealt with the apparition by praying all the harder. Another
time at the Capo di Bove, as he was walking along praying,
no less than three devils showed themselves to him at once.
On that occasion, so Bacci tells the story, he made game of
them; and to be mocked, as we know on the assurance of
the great St. Thomas More, who just about this time was
laying down his head on the block in the Tower of London,
to be mocked is what the devil, the proud spirit, can endure least.[1]

Other things were more dangerous. Sportive young men
with a perverted sense of humor thought it might be amusing to find out whether the virtue of the young saint would
be proof against what they considered a real test. Two of
them managed on some pretext to get him into a house in
which they shut him in a room with a couple of prostitutes.
All that happened was that the women were abashed to
hear the fervor of Philip's prayers. Another time — it is not
clear whether it was during this period or his early days as
a priest — a famous courtezan named Cesarea attempted his
seduction. When he fled from her, running pell-mell down
the stairs, she threw a stool at his head. Probably it was

---

[1] While we do hear now and then of similar apparitions in Philip's life,
they grew far less frequent as he grew older and holier. Moreover, in all
this something must be allowed to the imagination of the early biographers.
Bacci does not seem to see that there is anything even a little ludicrous
in his account of the devil appearing to Philip in the form of a small boy
holding a handkerchief to his nose and making fun of him. Nor does the
possibility occur to him that it might really have been a prankish boy and
not the devil at all.

because of these encounters that, until relatively late in life, he had as little to do with women as possible. To the end his distinctive work — the work of the Oratory — was exclusively for men. And though he did come to accept a number of women as penitents, many of these were the wives or sisters of his disciples.

The work of the Oratory, however, was as yet far off, and it was approached only by gradual stages. Philip continued to live with Caccia and to tutor his sons, but beyond that he had no definite occupation. He was still a hermit, withdrawn from all human contacts. Not even when, about two years after arriving in Rome, he began to study theology and philosophy, did he have the slightest idea of preparing himself for the priesthood. If he studied, says Bacci, it was "in order the better to understand heavenly things."

To have been able to take these courses he must be presumed to have obtained money somehow. Perhaps for a time he accepted a clerkship in one of the business houses in the Banchi. Perhaps Caccia pressed upon him enough to pay his fees and to buy books. But the money, wherever its source, could not have been much. For we hear of Philip reading on the porches of churches in the moonlight, because he was too poor to be able to afford a candle to light his pages. During the day he was to be seen walking out to the Campagna with his day's provisions of a roll and a book carried in his hermit's hood. In this way he studied for two years.

About Philip as a student we hear something quite definite. At the University of the Sapienza, where he went for philosophy, his professors were Cesare Jacomelli, afterwards Bishop of Belcastro in Calabria and one of the theologians at the Council of Trent, and Alfonso Ferri, whom Paul III had brought from Naples to open a school of sur-

gery. For theology Philip went to the Augustinians, where
Alessandro Stradella, the future Bishop of Nepi, was his
teacher. A fellow-student, the Alessandro Butio who was
later accounted among the most distinguished philosophers
of his day, was to say that Philip was one of the best students in his class. But Philip himself confessed to Francesco Zazzara "that he had studied little, and that he had
not been able to learn much because he was occupied with
prayers and other spiritual exercises."

That we may take as quite literally true. In the lecture-
room at Sant' Agostino there hung a Crucifix which so dis-
tracted him that he would weep and sigh instead of fixing
his attention on what the professor was explaining. He was,
in fact, a mystic and not a scholar. But those who met him
in later years and expected to find a simple old priest without much learning were surprised at the acuteness of his
mind and the range of his information. In spite of this, it
would be idle to try to make out that Philip Neri ever became a finished scholar. He was really an extremely clever
man, capable of making what little he had learned go a
very long way. So when Alessandro Sauli, the General of
the Barnabites, and other learned men testified to Philip's
knowledge they were actually testifying to his native ability. He did not study much; he could not have studied much.
At the very utmost we can account for three years during
which he followed lectures — and more likely it was only
two years. And as all that time he was making his pilgrimages to the Seven Churches and spending his nights,
more often than not, praying in the catacombs, his attendance in the class-room can hardly have been other than
desultory.

The fact that about 1537 he ceased attending these lectures shows two things. One was that he had never had any

intention of becoming a priest, or he would have persisted. The other was that his studies had so enriched his mind that he felt that his purposes had already been served. He had gone to the lectures "the better to understand heavenly things." He now had enough to meditate on for years. Scholarship for its own sake was nothing to him.

Any other man would have kept his books. Not so with Philip. Having no further use for them, he at once sold them and gave the money to the poor. Capecelatro can find only one similar case among all the saints. It was that of St. Dominic. But Dominic sold his books, not because he did not need them, but in order to relieve those in want; Philip sold his books because he found he had reached a point where books were distracting him from God. It was a further step in his pursuit of an absolute poverty.

The Abbé Ponnelle makes at this point an interesting conjecture. It is that the struggling young student who was afterwards to be Cardinal Sirleto and librarian of the Vatican bought Philip's little library. It may be so. Such a surmise is surely harmless enough. But there is no secure foundation for it. All we positively know is that Philip Neri, after having studied a short time in the schools, decided to study no more. He had his room in Caccia's house. He had his daily roll of bread. "Bread and olives, olives and bread" — with these he was content. Now he could give himself completely to the contemplation of the divine.

Had he gone any further as a student he might have done some damage to that strange vocation of his. And yet he was still in the dark as to what that vocation was to be. All that he saw for the moment was that he must stop studying, as study was a distraction to him and as God was a distraction to study. With that decision he had reached another turning-point in his life.

Chapter Four

FIRE FROM HEAVEN

FOR a while Philip simply returned to his way of life as it had been before he began to study at Sant' Agostino and the Sapienza. If we suppose that he left the class-rooms some time in 1537, that would have given him a clear year of recollection, unbroken except for the instruction he gave to Caccia's two sons and the groups of the poor in the porches of the churches. In the hood of his hermit's habit as he walked out to the catacomb of St. Sebastian there was no longer any book for reading. It might contain a roll, his food for the day. That concession he had to make to his bodily needs. For the rest it was prayer, day and night.

But in 1538 the first sign of Philip's distinctive work appeared, though, even then, no clear indication was given of what was to follow. In that year, says Bacci, he started "to go about the squares, shops, schools, and sometimes even the banks, talking with all sorts of persons in a most engaging way about spiritual things." Never, of course, had he been the least morose or melancholy, though he had withdrawn from the world, but not even as yet did he give full rein to that famous affability of his. But already his charm was able to win people to himself and to God. "Well, my brothers," was his favorite opening question, "when shall we begin to do good?" This marked the first stage of his apostolate. The period of his personal preparation was not by any means over; but to what it was leading now began to appear.

This does not mean that he diminished his prayers or even that he ceased making his pilgrimages to the Seven Churches or spending his nights in the catacombs. It was, in fact, in the catacombs that something extraordinary was to happen to him before many years were over. But now along with prayer there went active work for the winning of souls.

His special technique seems, however, to have been at this time undeveloped. Affable as he was, we do not hear of his venturing upon the jests and practical jokes that were so conspicuous in his later life, though, of course, such things may have occurred without having been recorded. What may be described as the eccentricities of Philip were incidents related of him during the process for his beatification, and naturally the witnesses are nearly all people who knew him only in his old age. It would appear that in his youth these things were not greatly in evidence. The old man could go up at a solemn moment to the Swiss Guard and play with his magnificent beard, and be thought delightful for doing so; had the young man attempted anything of the kind he would probably have been instantly knocked down. And the priest was free to impose fantastic penances upon his disciples, where the layman, who was only one of a crowd of obscure hermits wandering the streets, had to act with circumspection. We may reasonably suppose, therefore, that there was a side of Philip that remained merely in potentiality at this time.

Moreover, we should remember that Philip always showed the most exquisite tact. There is no case recorded of anyone resenting the way Philip treated him, though he showed his whimsicality to cardinals and even to some of the popes themselves. And he was careful to impose the quainter sort of mortification — by which he made his penitents turn themselves into laughing-stocks — only upon those who, he knew, would willingly obey. The majority of his disciples were never asked to do anything absurd because Philip divined that, in their case, it would not be advisable. He had a delicate sense as to just how far he could go. At this stage his later technique would have been out of place. An easy naturalness, gaiety, cheerfulness, all-embracing kindness — these he used; but with the already sufficiently sportive clerks of the banks and warehouses he had to refrain from anything more than a little light-hearted chaffing in return for the somewhat rougher chaffing we may be sure the hermit received from them.

But if at first they laughed at him, he soon made himself immensely popular among them because of his humor, his good humor, and his readiness always to take a hand in their games of piastrella. And if there were some who ridiculed him, there were others — like the Frenchman Louis Ames, who was connected with the custom-house — who recognised at once that this strange young man was a remarkable person, a genius, perhaps a saint.

Philip had several advantages to start with, in addition to his personal attractiveness. He was a Florentine, and many of the banks and commercial houses were exclusively manned by Florentines who, during the pontificates of two Medici popes, had come to have a favored position in Rome. They were a "nation," and they inhabited their own quarter of the city, at once a clannish and convivial set. Philip, as a Florentine, was, from the outset, acceptable to them. Moreover, he was vouched for by Caccia, who as director-general of the custom-house, was an important personage. Yet while these facts served to obtain Philip a hearing, they would not of themselves alone have secured his standing. That was obtained only because these smart and sometimes raffish young men — not to be taken in by another young man, however plausible — soon came to see that everything about Philip was thoroughly genuine. Even those who began by looking upon him as an oddity were in short order captivated.

Perhaps the best proof of this is in the fact that when Prospero Crivelli, the cashier of one of the principal banks in the city — that of the Cavalcanti — was in trouble, it was to Philip that he went for advice, though Crivelli must have been the considerably older man. Because his bank went in for usurious contracts, and because he himself was in an amorous entanglement, his confessor, Father Giovanni Polanco, the secretary to St. Ignatius, refused to give him absolution until he rectified his way of life. He wished to be a Christian; he did not have the resolution to do what needed to be done. But he knew that the queer, likeable, young Florentine was a saint. Would not Philip pray for him? Philip listened to his story and in return spoke of the love of God in such a way that Crivelli was deeply moved. "And now go," he said; "I will pray so much that you will give up your occasion of sin." Not long afterwards the bank cashier was able to go to Polanco and make such a confession that he received the hitherto refused absolution. He became one of Philip's most devoted friends and ever afterwards lived a life that gave the greatest edification.

Crivelli's case attracted a good deal of attention because of the important position he held. It occurred in 1547. But both before and after that date Philip effected many other conversions of a similar sort in much the same circles. He made it his business to seek out not merely well-disposed, though weak, men of the stripe of Crivelli, but men of depraved life, men for whose reformation all hope had been abandoned.

On the other hand, there were men Philip encountered among the business offices who became priests because of him. Of these Teseo Raspa and Enrico Pietra are typical. So closely did he attach them to himself that they even went to live in the same community with him when he became a priest. As for those who joined religious orders under his influence, St. Ignatius used to grumble that Philip Neri was like the bell that called men to church without ever leaving its belfry. It seemed that Philip was resolved to live and die a layman.

About the same time that he began to work among the banks and offices of the business section, he also began to frequent the hospitals. This second activity of his was less original than the first, for it was what most devout souls did, at any rate from time to time. Among them all, the work was somewhat haphazard; people did it when they felt like it or had the leisure. When they did not go, the hapless patients in the hospitals — patients indeed they were in those days! — often got no attention at all.

Philip did what he could. He made beds and swept floors and brought meals to the sick and even got them special food from outside. But that was about as far as his material ministrations could extend. To do this was a real and useful mortification for him, as he was inclined to be extraordinarily fastidious; the stench of the wards and the general dirt was almost more than could be borne by a man who could not bring himself to drink out of a glass that was used by other people, however thoroughly washed it might be. For the patients themselves his greatest service was a spiritual one. If they were dying, he would try to find a priest to give them the last sacraments, for there were no chaplains regularly employed in the hospitals. And if a priest was not to be obtained he would stay with the dying himself — sometimes days and nights on end — helping them to dispose their souls for death. Later in his life he inspired one of his penitents, St. Camillus de Lellis, to found an order whose sole work was that of looking after the sick. At this stage he went himself and took a few friends with him sometimes, and, when he became a priest, he made a point of packing off some fine young gentlemen to perform nauseating works of corporal mercy in the wards. Yet, because of its lack of system, work of this sort could not have been particularly efficient. The world was waiting for the organizations that St. Camillus set up in Rome and St. Vincent de Paul in Paris.

It was probably at this time that Philip met the first Jesuits. Their work at the outset consisted mostly of preaching in the streets and helping in the hospitals. Ignatius had not yet made his plans for world conquest — plans that necessitated his withdrawal from his early activities so that he might sit down at the centre of an ever-widening web to direct the men he was to send all over Europe and to India. But the tradition of hospital work is still preserved in the Society, at any rate to the extent that it is still recognised by Jesuits as a distinct form of preparation for attaining the true spirit of their vocation. Though the nature of these activities is, of course, somewhat changed by changed circumstances, they at least bear their origins in mind to this extent.

Tacchi-Venturi, who is the chief authority on the early history of the Society, makes the conjecture that Philip got acquainted with the Jesuits during 1538 or 1539, just when he was beginning his active apostolate and while they were still free-lancing in Rome. He supposes, too, that it was St.

Frances Xavier who introduced Philip to Ignatius. Certainly Philip knew Francis, and the day was to come, after the publication of the great missionary's letters, when he was himself all on fire to follow in his footsteps.[1] Their acquaintanceship, however, must have been brief, for Francis left Rome early in 1540. Philip was to see more of Ignatius.

The Abbé Ponnelle suggests that it may have been this contact with Ignatius that led Philip to regularise his life. Certainly the Jesuits soon came to see that unsystematised work had small results. With the practicality that characterised them, they ruled out such things, along with obligatory imposition of numerous specific penances: "fasts, disciplines, bare heads and feet, colored dress, strange food, penances, hair shirts, and other macerations." For this was part of the minutes that Cardinal Contarini read to Pope Paul III on their famous walk together in September 3, 1539. The Ignatian influence would have been all in the direction of putting Philip to some regular employment.

On the other hand, there was another influence Philip encountered — either during this period or a little later — which would have operated against the Jesuits. Philip probably already knew Francesco Marsuppini, and who acted as his confessor after 1558, and Marsuppini was a man who had been a Jesuit and, in a highly critical mood, had left them. But we have no reason to suppose that Philip was in the least affected by Marsuppini's opinions; we do know that it was Philip who claimed to have sent Ignatius the first recruits he obtained in Italy.

There has been some controversy as to whether Ignatius tried to draw him into the Society, or as to whether Philip

---

[1] Even then, however, his plan was that of going out to India as an unattached missionary. He never showed any wish to join the Jesuits, or, for that matter, any other order.

applied for admission and was refused. The argument
would seem to be idle. No two saints could be more unlike
in their character, aims, and methods than these. Ignatius
would have seen at a glance that the inspired individualist,
whatever else he might be, was not a potential Jesuit. And
for the reason that Philip did not want to enter the Society,
neither did he want to join the Dominicans or Capuchins,
despite his friendship with those orders, or even to become
a secular priest. There still lay before him a dozen years in
Rome during which he was to continue in his old way,
wandering between his room in Caccia's house and the catacombs, although he had now modified his life to the extent
of talking about God to young businessmen or making himself useful in the hospitals. All the indications were that he
meant to go on in the same way to the end.

It is clear that whatever external activities he had taken
up did not in the least diminish the intensity of his interior
preoccupations. For now we come to what is the central
experience of Philip's life and the seal that was set upon it.
About the way that experience manifested itself there cannot be a shadow of doubt, for this was something physical
and, as such, observed by thousands of people. The violent
tremblings of his body that resulted made Philip a marked
man for the fifty years he had still to live, and after his
death an autopsy was performed which showed that he
had a bodily peculiarity; two of his ribs were broken and
arched over his heart so as to give the appearance of a
tumor. That much is absolutely certain. The explanation of
the fact, as Ludwig von Pastor points out, is one that the
historian should less than anyone else be called upon to give.

What happened, according to Philip's own account, was
this: It was just before Pentecost in the year 1544 and
Philip was praying in the catacomb of San Sebastiano. His

mystical exaltation had already often reached such a pitch
that he had been obliged to cry out to God, "No more, no
more, or I shall die!" Often he had been filled with fire
that obliged him to bare his breast to cool it; often he
had fallen to the ground overwhelmed. But this time a
climax was reached. Now there came upon him, instead of
the tongues of flame that lighted upon the heads of those
in the first Pentecost, a ball of fire which, to quote Bacci,
"entered his mouth and lodged in his breast." He was hurled
to the floor of the narrow tunnel in which he was praying
and when, after a while, he recovered himself, he felt that
his whole body was shaking. Putting his hand to his left
side, he found there a swelling as large as a man's fist.
Neither then nor at any time afterwards was it attended
with the slightest pain; on the contrary it gave him a sense
of ineffable joy, though it frequently so exhausted him as
to bring on mysterious illnesses. In spite of these, he lived
to be eighty and was active to the end. What people could
not but notice was that, whenever he was taken by any
emotion, the hammer strokes of his heart shook the bed or
chair on which he sat and sometimes even the whole room.

Yet there was nothing pathological about his condition.
His trembling was always completely under his own control; at any moment he could stop it. As Philip himself told
Cardinal Federigo Borromeo, "I do not ordinarily do so,
so as not to distract myself from prayer by any deliberate
act of my will." In short, his violent palpitations were an
outward sign of his fervor and occurred only when he gave
that fervor full rein. They came upon him when he was
saying Mass, and often when he was giving absolution in
confession, and when he was praying. It was also a most
powerful means of conveying to others a sense of God's
grace. Tiberio Ricciardelli and Marcello Vitelleschi, both of

whom were canons in Rome, were among those who testified at Philip's Process that he put their temptations to
flight merely by drawing them against his breast. They, like
Philip himself, were quite sure that there was something
supernatural about his physical state. He did his best to
conceal it by carrying a large handkerchief on his left side
to cover his malformation.

This strange thing has often been compared to the stigmata of St. Francis of Assisi. And indeed it was, just as
much as the stigmata, the crown and climax of the mystical
state in which he had been for ten years. But it might be
noted that there have been at least a hundred well-authenti-
cated cases of the stigmata — several of them in our own
generation — and that there has never been more than one
case of a heart so inflamed with love of God as to break the
ribs of the encasing body.

It is instructive to note that this occurrence made no
change in Philip's life. For seven years he was to go on
just as before, perhaps with an ever increasing sense of
union with God but with no departure from his routine of
prayer in the catacombs and the pilgrimages to the Seven
Churches and the visits to the Banchi and the hospitals. No
vision appeared to him; no voice from heaven spoke. He
remained what he had been. Left to himself, he would never
have been anything else.

He was not left to himself. The first move in a new direction — and a quite unconscious one — was made when, on
August 16, 1548, more than four years after the coming to
him of fire from heaven, Philip joined with Persiano Rosa,
his confessor, in founding the Confraternity of Pilgrims and
Convalescents. That was not its name as yet; it is doubtful
whether it had any name at all at the outset, for the pilgrims and the convalescents did not come into their plans

until 1550. All that happened at first was that, after a short period when the meetings were held at the Church of San Girolamo, to which Rosa was attached, the gatherings of the little society were transferred to San Salvatore in Campo. There a group of twelve or fifteen men met for pious exercises. Their object may have been to establish on a small scale and in an unambitious way something resembling the Oratory of the Divine Love. More likely it was merely one more instance of an attempt to revive the Italian Confraternity of the Middle Ages. In the unpretentious conferences of the little group we may discern the germ of Philip's Oratory, but we may be sure that at the time nobody had any more definite purpose than giving one another some help in the spiritual life, especially in the form of encouragement in the frequenting of the sacraments.

The main distinctive feature of this confraternity was that it introduced into Rome from Milan, where it had originated in 1527, the Forty Hours' Devotion. This devotion was practiced on the first Sunday of every month and during Holy Week. On such occasions, strangely enough, it was not Persiano Rosa, the priest, but Philip Neri, the layman, who was the life and soul of everything. He never left the church but would every now and then preach a short sermon. It was all very simple and familiar, something that was hardly formal enough to be called a sermon in the ordinary sense. And all those present, even those who went to make fun of the curious spectacle of a layman preaching in church, were touched. Philip was not a priest, but he was so obviously a saint that everyone came to take his preaching for granted. Rosa apparently did no more than exercise general supervision and, of course, expose the Blessed Sacrament for adoration. As each man in his turn reached the end of his hour of watching, Philip would ring a little bell and say, "Now your hour of prayer is over, but not the time for doing good."

It may well have been this that put into Rosa's mind the conviction that Philip had a vocation to be a priest. He probably often spoke about it to him before he succeeded in breaking down his reluctance. As Philip said many times afterwards, "he had wished to serve God as a layman and to be neither priest nor confessor." But Rosa persisted in maintaining his pressure. Meanwhile every month the exercises of the Confraternity were held, attended only by a small group of poor unlettered men. Once, however, a band of thirty smart young clerks and silversmiths came into the church in a body to jeer at the preacher. That time they found more than they had bargained for; all were converted. It was so with others who came to scoff.

There was no very definite organization about this confraternity, but there was at least a group that could be formed into an organization. The opportunity for this, and a need, occurred during the jubilee of 1550. For, when a large influx of pilgrims began to pour into Rome, the Confraternity, observing how many of the pilgrims arrived weary and without any place to go, took a house and provided what shelter and hospitality it could afford. The members of the Confraternity all wore a kind of hermit's robe and hood — of red to signify charity. This gave them a distinguishing uniform; it also masked them and made them anonymous.

The Confraternity started a piece of social work that was in later years to have a good deal of importance. But at this time its resources were pitifully meagre and the members could not have been seriously thinking that they would be able to provide for all the thousands of pilgrims who were arriving; at best, they could have expected to do a little for a chance few. They looked upon these through the eyes of their own humble mysticism, seeing in them a means of receiving Jesus Christ who had not where to lay His head. Their piety was so contagious that even the cook they employed — a man of whom nobody expected anything of the kind — "arrived at such perfection," says Bacci, "that he often went out at night, when it was clear, and fixing his eyes on the heavens, was sweetly absorbed in the contemplation of divine things."

The work the members did, however, was not only of benefit to them in their spiritual life, it was also surprisingly successful from the point of view of those for whom it was done. The small house they had taken proved almost at once inadequate for their purposes, and another had to be found, though even there they could provide no more than a dozen beds. Then the popular imagination took fire, and people came forward to help the Confraternity. The headquarters of the Pilgrims was moved from San Salvatore in Campo to the large establishment of the Trinità dei Pellegrini. No less than five hundred people were being taken care of every day, being given at least a light meal at the Confraternity's hostel. By the time of the next jubilee — 1575 — it gave shelter to no less than 144,913 pilgrims and distributed 365,132 meals, a prodigious achievement. At that time some of the most illustrious people in Rome, cardinals and members of the nobility — including the great Duke of Colonna himself — and even Pope Gregory XIII waited upon the poor pilgrims at their meals. Clement VIII, another of Philip's friends, and his successors continued the tradition.

There was an important outcome to this. After the departure of the pilgrims at the end of 1550 — and as there would not be another jubilee for twenty-five years — the house taken by the Confraternity was put to use for convalescents. Philip had been keeping up his visits to the hospitals and had noticed that the poor were often discharged so soon that they had a serious relapse. He therefore had the idea of giving them a chance for complete recovery in the Confraternity's hostel. How he managed to finance these undertakings is a mystery, especially as there was nobody connected with the original group who had any money. But presumably the people of wealth and position whom he had got to know during the jubilee now came forward with offers of help. At any rate this second work was established and the Confraternity took as its full name that of the Pilgrims and Convalescents.

Cardinal Capecelatro remarks that this was the first public work of the saint. Yet even this was hardly more than a work initiated by him; his formal association with it, except as an honorary member, ceased after the first year. Philip was no Vincent de Paul, no organizer of charity, no prompter of any kind of project. He was simply an improvisor. Aware that something had to be done, he did it, and then resigned the charge to those he found ready to take his place. But at least he should get the credit for starting the famous Confraternity.

Though he was now working with an organized body, he also performed many purely personal acts of charity, things that of their nature could best be done outside of the Society. It was during the jubilee year that he heard of an old man of noble birth who was in destitution. Most people would have tried to help him through the agency that had just been set up; but not Philip. In his delicacy he feared that such a person might resent it if his condition were made known; therefore he went to see him secretly at dead of night, taking with him food and money. In the same way he assisted students who needed money for books or fees for their courses; and to girls whose virtue was in danger because of their poverty he also contrived to bring relief. Here he was like that St. Nicholas of Bari whose bags of gold, thrown through the open window to young women in similar danger, created the legend that has turned him into our Santa Claus. To nobody did Philip ever refuse anything — which shows him to have been a most unenlightened sociologist. He actually believed that charity should depend upon a person's necessity and not upon his deserts. That he was able to supply the needs of so many shows that the friends he had made were now making him their almoner. We hear of no wealthy benefactors, but a host of small donations served just as well. It was by such means that the hostel of the Confraternity was kept going. Even so, people wondered where he obtained the money he gave away; it was sometimes surmised during his life that it must have come to him miraculously. For it was noticed that he never asked anybody for anything and yet never lacked something to give.

All this external activity, however, began to create a doubt in his mind. He thought that what he was doing was distracting him from his habit of contemplation, and he wondered whether he ought not to return to the solitary prayer that had been his during his first two years in Rome. At the same time it never seems to have occurred to him to bury himself entirely in the catacombs or in a cave on a mountainside. Some deep intuition made him see that his work was to be in Rome. There was no temptation that the hermit should forsake the streets.

Whatever doubts he had regarding this matter served in the end to remove all doubts. If there was a period of hesitation, he was never afterwards to hesitate again. In the years to come this mystic, this ecstatic, was always at anybody's beck and call. It was perfectly understood that he might at any moment be summoned from prayer if anybody wished to see him. For this was, as he often said, only to leave God for God. He was to be the most sociable contemplative the world has ever seen, one who discovered a way of continuing to pray even when he was talking with the greatest vivacity. In him the vocations of Mary and Martha were perfectly joined. Invaded though he was by all kinds of demands, never did his mystical life suffer.

He must have been praying for guidance when he had that vision of St. John the Baptist about which in old age he told Cardinal Federigo Borromeo. But the terms used by the Cardinal, when he related the story during the Process for Philip's beatification, do not necessarily indicate an actual vision. Such visions were, indeed, to come to him; this one could have been merely a dream. In any event he recognised the saint for whom all Florentines had so deep a veneration. Though no word was spoken, Philip somehow knew that he was intended to live in Rome not solely for his own sanctification but for the salvation of souls.

Perhaps he told Persiano Rosa of this vision of his. It is certain that Rosa, who was his confessor, tried all the harder about this time to persuade Philip that he ought to become a priest. Nevertheless, Philip held back. He did his best to convince Rosa that he was unfit for such a high calling and that he believed he should continue to serve God as a layman. In turn, the confessor, while approving his humility, argued that this was a matter which Philip should allow him to decide. He had observed how effective Philip was as a preacher, and he knew that such unauthorised preaching would, in all likelihood, not be permitted indefinitely. The new reforming spirit in the Church, which was

now especially active in Rome because of the Council of
Trent, was already bringing about a greater degree of centralization. Free-lance evangelists and wandering hermits
were not being encouraged. The efforts of all devout souls
were to be canalized and directed. Therefore Philip had
better become a priest. In the end Rosa abandoned all attempts at argument and gave his penitent a direct and positive order.

It was only in obedience to his confessor that Philip
yielded. No vision appeared to him this time, no voice was
heard. St. John the Baptist did not come again. There was
no need for that. The cheerful and sensible Persiano Rosa
spoke with God's authority. And Philip — still the good
Pippo — did what he was told.

He was now nearly thirty-six, and for half that number of
years he had been a saint. But there was a certain amount
of danger that he might develop by degrees into a religious
eccentric, of whom there were already too many. In any
case there was much more that he could do than he had
so far done. Persiano Rosa perceived that the time had now
come for doing it. Philip bowed before his insistence. As
Ponnelle puts it, he was made a priest by force.

The decision once made, holy orders were quickly conferred upon him. In those days there was no definite train-
ing for the priesthood; though seminaries were projected,
they had not yet come into being. Many a man was ordained
on hardly more than his knowing enough Latin to say Mass.
As things went, Philip had been well trained. Though he
had shut up his books of philosophy and theology thirteen
years ago, his memory of what he had learned at the
Sapienza and Sant' Agostino was still vivid. All that he had
to do was, under Rosa's direction, to make himself acquainted with the ceremonies of the Mass. Among the books

that had belonged to him and that are still preserved in
Rome is a little tattered volume whose condition shows how
thoroughly Philip must have thumbed it while waiting for
ordination. It is a manual of instructions for the priest-to-be.

The several orders were conferred on him in a succession
unusually rapid. In March, 1551, on different days, he was
given the tonsure, minor orders, and the subdiaconate. On
Holy Saturday he was made deacon in the basilica of St.
John Lateran; and on May 23 that year the same bishop
who had conferred all the other orders, Giovanni Lunelli
of Sebaste, ordained him priest in the Church of San Tomaso
in Parione.

Philip's was an exceptional case. His ordination came
relatively late. And though many men, both before and
since, have been ordained when they were still older, as a
rule they had not had anything like Philip's antecedent life,
one that had been wholly an unconscious preparation for
the priesthood. He would have preferred, had his own in-
clinations been consulted, to have remained like the St.
Francis of Assisi he so admired and whom he resembled in
many ways — one completely devoted to God's service, but
as a layman. It was not to be. His great work lay ahead of
him. That he was brought to perform it we owe to the dis-
cernment of Persiano Rosa.

His priesthood must have come on about the seventh
anniversary of the descent upon him of fire from heaven in
the catacomb of San Sebastiano, possibly on the very day
itself. We are told that in seven years the constitution of
the body so changes that not a single particle of what was
there at the beginning remains at the end. Physically that
may be so, though even physically the former characteristics
are left. Philip still had the enlarged heart that had so
nearly burst from his body and that made him shake so

violently whenever he was seized by religious fervor. Mentally and morally, of course, there had been no change whatever. It would be hard to think of anybody who from youth to extreme old age was more of a single piece. All that ever occurred was a development and a further enrichment. We may well linger, in company with Cardinal Capecelatro, over the beautiful figure of Philip Neri as a layman: "for, in some respects, it wins and attaches our hearts more than even his grander and more imposing presence as a priest."

Chapter Five

THE ROOM TO WHICH EVERYONE
WENT

IT WAS perhaps fortunate for Philip that he began his work during the pontificate of Julius III. For, though this was a period of reform, it was that of reform exercised with more discretion and moderation than was shown by Paul IV when he came to the throne five years later. The election of Cardinal del Monte was an apparent accident. He was a dark horse of whom nobody had been thinking, and he was put forward at one of the longest of conclaves and one very full of political intrigue.

Reginald Pole the Englishman, who had the backing of the Emperor Charles V, came within one vote of being elected, and would have been elected for a certainty had he not refused to do anything to further his own cause. The other candidates who were without his scruples eventually killed off one another, and the exhausted cardinals decided upon the easy-going Julius. He was obliged to continue the reform that had already begun; he was far from being the man to have initiated it. The atmosphere of Rome therefore was one in which an innovator could follow his own devices without arousing too much suspicion. It might have been quite different for Philip had the terrible Paul IV been elected instead.

Quite possibly one of the inducements held out to Philip

51

when Persiano Rosa was trying to persuade him to become a
priest was that he could take up his quarters in the house
attached to the church of San Girolamo della Carità, where
Rosa himself lived and where he would have been in a
position to have arranged matters for Philip. It may be
surmised that he pointed out that at no place in all Rome
could Philip be more independent, for he well understood
that this was a man who could do his work only if he were
allowed to do it in his own way. At all events, it was here
that Philip went immediately after his ordination. Had he
been ordained a few years later, it could only have been
on a benefice — which would have meant a sacrifice of his
freedom.

The church itself was, according to tradition, built upon
the site of St. Paula's palace, where she had entertained St.
Jerome. And the house had been a Franciscan monastery
until 1536, when the friars had transferred themselves to
San Bartolomeo in Isola. Then their cloister and the little
hospital connected with it had been taken over by the Archconfraternity of Charity which Cardinal Guilio de' Medici
(afterwards Clement VII) had founded and endowed in
1519. This confraternity was a kind of clearing-house for
various social and charitable activities. It operated under
the control of a committee, consisting mostly of laymen.
These were the virtual owners of the place and the priests
were no more than the chaplains of the society. The point
is important and should be remembered.

Thirteen priests were employed at this church and others
who had no definite obligations were allowed to reside in
the adjoining monastery. Those among them who were chaplains were, of course, paid a salary; the others were given
nothing but their room and board and were obliged to

subsist on what they could pick up by officiating on special occasions. Philip must have been referring to such clerics (who abounded in Rome) when, at the end of his life, he told the members of his Congregation that they were not to consider themselves a whit better than those poor priests who followed funerals with greasy breviaries tucked under their arms.

The burial of the poor was, in fact, one of the purposes of the Confraternity. But it also distributed charity, especially to those who were too genteel to approach other organizations; and it organized the visiting of the prisons and made itself responsible for obtaining legal defence for prisoners who had no means. This last had become the most prominent of its functions; through it the Confraternity had grown to be extremely influential.

It must be borne in mind that the priests residing there were employees and exercised no control over the activities of the Confraternity. On the other hand, effective control could be exercised only over those to whom a salary was given, though even these appear to have had no duties except those of hearing confessions and of saying eight Masses on Sundays and holydays of obligation. With so many priests at hand, those duties could not have been onerous. Philip Neri seemingly was one of the resident clerics who were not bound to any obligation. He was therefore one of those who received no salary.

Capecelatro offers the absence of salary as one more proof of Philip's love of poverty. Actually it was rather due to his determination to maintain his independence. For, as Ponnelle shows, he did take the place of Francesco Marsuppini in 1552. But it was only for a year. After that there appeared an entry in the diary of the house: "The Floren-

tine priest Philip has for the future renounced all salary for
his services, offering to give them as he chooses." While he
did more work than any other man in the house, he did not
wish to be tied down. It was to keep his freedom, to offer
his services as he chose, that he sacrificed his salary.

Philip was able to do this all the more successfully because the priests in the house, all of whom were of the
secular clergy, had no superior but, as Bacci puts it, observed only the order of seniority. As we shall see, there
was some exaggeration in saying that "they lived a tranquil
and almost heavenly life," although that may have been
true of the majority. There was no particular rule that they
had to observe, nor did they even take their meals in
common.

Such an arrangement perfectly suited the individualistic
Philip. The system, or the lack of system, however, worked
well enough for Capecelatro to see in this informal mode
of life something that suggested the plan for the subsequent
Congregation of the Oratory. But it is worth noting that,
even after he had founded that religious institute, Philip
contrived to be personally independent of it, that for a long
time he lived apart from his own subjects and that, when
at last he consented to reside with them, he retired into the
most remote corner of the house he could find and generally
took his meals in his own room.

By that time this idiosyncrasy of his was understood and
respected. For he was seen to be at the same moment the
most accessible of men, and the most aloof. He was jealous
of what little privacy he managed to obtain precisely
because he got so little of it. Unless some positive duty
called, he wished to be alone so as to live his mystical life.
What looked like a piece of eccentricity was actually practicality. But we can hardly be surprised if, during his first

years at San Girolamo, some people saw in this nothing except eccentricity.

They were all the more sure that Philip was being eccentric because San Girolamo already contained an elderly priest who really was an eccentric, even though he did a valuable work, a work which prepared the way for Philip. This was Buonsignore Cacciaguerra, whose speciality was the promoting of frequent Holy Communion, just as Philip's speciality was the promoting of frequent confession. The two men were all the more of a complement to each other because in character and in personal history they stood in startling contrast.

Cacciaguerra wrote his autobiography, which was afterwards rewritten in the third person; and what he had to relate would appear to be incredible did it not also happen to be true. Born in 1494 at Siena of a wealthy family, he built up a still larger fortune of his own and lived as Governor of Sicily in the most opulent splendor. Forty slaves, whites as well as blacks, attended him. So also did a swarm of flatterers and hangers-on, for whom daily banquets were provided as at a king's table. But none of them could swagger so insolently as Cacciaguerra himself. An almost insane touch comes out in the fact that, after he had worn a suit of clothes — and they were always of the richest materials — he cut it in pieces so that nobody else might wear it after him. He supplied himself, of course, with a succession of mistresses.

Yet with all this he did not altogether give up the practice of religion. At Easter he always went to confession and Communion. Then he resolved to leave his sins, but every time found that his desire for conversion was something that he was not yet prepared to follow. With remorse he would return to his mistress and his carousing companions, though the remorse would now and then make him act in such a way as to suggest a saint, as when he carried a beggar home and served him at table with his own hands.

Time after time this sort of incident happened, until one Easter Cacciaguerra heard a step behind him. Turning around, he saw Christ with a rope round His neck and staggering under His cross. "My son," he heard, "see how thou art treating Me! Do not drive Me from thee." Yet not that time, nor even at the next Easter, when he saw the apparition again, did he finally turn from his sins. Instead he attempted to stifle compunction by fresh excesses.

By now he had squandered much of his wealth away. The rest disappeared in a series of trading disasters. He was captured by pirates and, after he had got away, received a wound in the face from an affair of honor — from which he emerged with little honor to himself. This disfigured him for life. A further disfigurement was caused by an ulcer which ate his mouth away. His family having turned against him by now, he could find shelter only with an aged Negress who had been one of his slaves.

At last he stripped himself of his vanities. By way of seeking a means for expressing his penitence he went on foot to the shrine of St. James at Compostella in Spain, calling himself, as had Ignatius, the "Pilgrim," and was led to the shrine bound by cords like a criminal. In spite of this there was a time when he was all but overwhelmed by despair, believing his sins too heinous for God to forgive. Nevertheless he recovered peace. Then he lived a wandering life as a hermit, and signalised his strange conversion by working miracles, being especially effective in delivering those who were possessed. But the thing that mainly characterised him was that he received Holy Communion daily and that he exhorted others to do so. In 1547 he was ordained priest, when he was well past fifty, and in October, 1550, he came to settle at San Girolamo, existing solely on alms. There he gathered a group of disciples around him, still exhorting to daily or at least frequent Communion.

Such a man naturally attracted considerable attention, not because of his former life — about which most people could have known little — but chiefly because of his insistence on daily Communion. In those days to frequent the sacraments more often than twice a year was looked upon as an exhibition of piety that was almost pharisaically ostentatious.

It is instructive to note Cacciaguerra's case, because a century later rigor ran in the opposite direction. There was, of course, much more in Jansenism than its discouragement of frequent Communion, for that was no more than a deduction from more fundamental heresies which marked the emergence of Calvinism in a quasi-Catholic form. But the practical program of Jansenism was that of holding people back from frequent Communion on the ground that it was hardly conceivable that any soul could be in a state fit for the reception of the Eucharist. Such scrupulosity was taken as a mark of a delicate spirituality, whereas frequent communicants were stigmatised as lax. But if Cacciaguerra was anything but lax, he must be admitted to have shown an inclination to overstress a single point. The totality of Catholicism was in danger of being lost sight of when all the weight was thrown on fervor, especially a fervor that manifested itself, as it did among Cacciaguerra's disciples, as a taste for visions and ecstasies. What Cacciaguerra was doing badly needed to be balanced by the work that Philip was to do.

Even in Philip's case, it might, perhaps, be objected that the totality of Catholicism was not perfectly achieved. For his methods, too, laid great stress on personal fervor — certainly something very desirable — but sought to work up that fervor by novel means. Yet Philip can hardly be blamed if he did not avail himself to the full of the tradition of liturgical spirituality. That had largely frozen into routine, so much so that all the new movements of what is called the Counter-Reformation were disposed to fasten on this or that special devotion to the neglect of the liturgy as the normal and most efficacious means of developing a rounded Christian life. The *Opus Dei* was thought of as something performed by monks, and monasticism itself, at any rate in its older forms, as an anachronism. Probably enough, the times did call for a "shortening of the lines" for the sake of defence. Catholicism was made more "efficient" but at the same time grew less rich; its practice was narrowed so as to meet a dangerous crisis. Only now are we beginning to get over some of these effects of the Counter-Reformation.

But the question is a large one and cannot be dealt with adequately here. All that need be said is that probably only new methods in spirituality could have revived religion, even though those methods did tend to emphasise a part somewhat to the expense of the whole. If this objection can be raised at all against Philip, it should be raised very gently. Never did he — or for that matter, St. Ignatius, who may be considered as being mainly instrumental in giving the new tone to spiritual practice — in the least deny the value of the older sort of Catholic spirituality. And Philip remained a good deal closer to the traditions of the past than did most of the great leaders of his time. Comparing him with St. Ignatius, we see the founder of the Jesuits using as his most powerful weapon the Spiritual Exercises, whose purpose was to give a drill so intensive that they were conceived as enough to arm the soul for a life-long

service to God, while Philip's idea was that spiritual development was a gradual process, depending not on one decisive experience but on a day-by-day watchfulness and the
quiet operation of grace.[1]

That in this Philip — like St. Ignatius in another way —
was immensely effective will soon be evident. If Philip's
method had a weakness, it was that of inducing too great
a personal dependence upon himself. He could not be at
ease about anybody unless he saw him every day, wishing
even to hear his confession every day. The strength of his
method — and by this it must be judged — is that those who
did keep in contact with him had their spiritual lives mar-
vellously quickened. His success along his own lines was
phenomenal.

The first thing he had to do was to persuade people who
had been extremely lax — and this meant practically everybody — to go to confession. As soon as the church was
opened at daybreak Philip was in his confessional, remaining there until he said his Mass, which was usually at mid-
day. If no penitents came, he stayed near his confessional
reading or saying his office or reciting the rosary. That
people might know that a priest was available, he would
every now and then go outside and walk up and down in
front of the church. If they did not come to him, he was
ready to go to them — for a good confession was the start
of a reformed life.

His reputation soon spread. Not only did he hear confessions all morning from an early hour, but he was hearing confessions in his room until late at night. It often happened, too, that even before he went down to the church

---

[1] This, of course, St. Ignatius did not overlook. He provided not merely
a thorough two years' novitiate, for instance, but also a third year, known
as a tertianship, and taken after ordination.

at daybreak he had heard as many as forty confessions. To let the young men he was gathering around him know that no time was too early for them to come, he showed them where he put his key under the door; all that they had to do was to open it and go in. He would at once get out of bed to hear a confession. And whatever he might be doing during the day, he would instantly break off, if he was told that a penitent was waiting for him.

Bacci says that to hear confessions Philip "abandoned every other care." Indeed, at this period the hearing of confessions could have left him no time for anything else. Even his visits to the hospitals had to be discontinued for a while, though when he could not go himself he would send some of his disciples to take his place — especially those most certain to find a mortification in such work. From the day of his ordination until the day of his death Philip was primarily a confessor. Not even when he was sick would he cease hearing confessions, unless this was positively forbidden by his doctors. Even then he would, as likely as not, hear a few confessions while lying in bed. If he was told that he should not fatigue himself in this way, he answered simply, "But it is not a fatigue at all. It is rather a relief and recreation to me."

But though he was primarily a confessor, he was not by any means solely that. The work of the future Oratory was already beginning to develop, and this consisted in the giving of spiritual conferences. But these were intended to fit in with the hearing of confessions. The talks in his room to the group he had begun to gather around him were an extension of the confessional; he was able to say to a number what he did not have the time or opportunity to say to each individual. On the other hand, the confessional was his method of keeping up the devotion of this group.

As this was his way of preventing them from losing their fervor, it was necessary that they could be quite sure of finding him whenever they wanted him. The relationship between Philip and his disciples was perhaps the most personal and intimate that there has ever been in the history of the Church.

At first Philip was somewhat under Cacciaguerra's influence in laying a great stress upon the importance of frequent if not daily Communion. Later, however, it was his practice to make confession more frequent than Communion. His ideal was that he should have his penitents go to him every day; but he considered that, for most of them, Communion once a week was quite enough. In this there was no anticipation of the Jansenist rigor — for, even with the limitations he imposed, Philip's disciples were still encouraged to a frequency of Communion which was most exceptional in those days; it was rather that he sought, by holding them back, to increase their desire for the Holy Eucharist. If he refused his permission that they should go as often as they wished, it was by saying, "No, *thirsting* come ye to the waters." The Church, however, has made most clear in our day that it is precisely the love engendered by fervent daily Communion that most increases this thirst within the soul. Though Philip began by working as a kind of auxiliary to Cacciaguerra, he soon came to follow a somewhat divergent line of his own.

It was to hold his penitents together that Philip took his next step and invented for them those devotional exercises which came to be the distinguishing mark of the Oratory. They began in a very simple and unpretentious fashion. Believing that the time after the mid-day dinner was that in which those vivacious young men were most liable to get into mischief, he arranged that they should come to

him then. That they were able to do so, and to stay for the
greater part of the afternoon, makes one wonder when they
earned their living.

Yet with the exception of young Fabrizio de'Massimi, a
wealthy youth of sixteen, all had some occupation to which
they were supposed to attend. We know who they were
and what they did. Monte Zazzara conducted a perfumery
shop. Michele da Prato was a maker of hosiery. Simone
Grazzini was a nephew of the banker Buonsignori and employed by his uncle. Francesco and Sebastiano were two
young goldsmiths. One or two others, among whom was
Louis Ames, an Angevin employed at the custom-house,
came occasionally. But he and Massimi were the only members of the first group who were not Tuscans. All of them
seem to have had endless time to spare. For even allowing
for a certain amount of coming and going during the course
of the afternoon, Philip always had some of these men
around him then and also in the evening.

Though these all recognised, of course, that he was a very
good man, it did not at once dawn on them that he was a
saint. They thought of him rather as having inexhaustible
kind-heartedness; and it was this that attracted them. With
these seven or eight men he would talk in his room after
dinner and encourage them to talk. Almost before they realised what they were doing, some of them found that they
were, in effect, preaching little homilies, Philip's function
being mainly confined to prompting them or asking a question when the conversation flagged.

Yet, even at that early date, these men soon discovered
that there was something more extraordinary about Philip
than his gentleness and geniality. As he sat on his bed or
leaned against it they noticed that every now and then he
would become so moved with emotion that his eyes filled

with tears and that his body trembled so violently as to shake the whole room. Or if he was standing, it seemed to them sometimes that, in his strong fervor, his body was lifted from the ground a few inches into the air. Above all, they felt that when he embraced them, as he often did, there flowed out from him a spiritual warmth and light such as they had never known before. All this happened so frequently that they came to take it for granted in him.

There was no set method or program in these little gatherings. Sometimes Philip would read a page or two to them from a book — usually from Cassian or from a life of a saint, that of Blessed Colombini being most often drawn upon — and then he would invite comments. But sometimes he would propose a topic for consideration — never a point of formal theology, but some practical consideration. Whatever it was, however, the young men themselves did most of the talking. Philip sat there, his eyes shining, beaming upon them, and trying to draw them out. It was in this way that the Oratory began.

After an hour or two spent in this manner, the group of friends would go out for a walk, sometimes singing as they went. They might make a pilgrimage to St. Peter's or St. John Lateran, and afterwards drop in at the great friary of the Dominicans, the Minerva, to hear a sermon or to assist at Vespers. By this time probably some of those who had gone to Philip's room after dinner found that they had other matters to attend to; but others, now free, came to take their places. There were always a few young men who would go back to Philip's room and there — with the lamp turned low and throwing its beam only on a Crucifix — Philip would instruct them in the art of mental prayer. One of his first disciples, Simone Grazzini, has described these prayer meetings: "The Father prayed, and we saw his

intense fervor. His whole body was shaken, and he seemed
to tremble as he spoke with God, and, although the prayer
may have lasted an hour, it seemed very short to us, and
we could have stopped there all night, so great was the
sweetness we felt."

One would think that even the harshest judgment would
not find any ground for criticism in these proceedings. Even
if we put out of our minds for the moment all the admiration Philip was soon to be accorded, all the recognition his
great work eventually obtained, these conversations and
walks and prayer meetings surely could have done nobody
any harm. I deliberately put it that way, so as to start with
the lowest estimate. On that range itself, one would suppose that Philip would have escaped criticism.

Perhaps he would have escaped it, had it not been for
Cacciaguerra. The first year at San Girolamo in fact passed
without any particular trouble; possibly because Philip's
visitors were as yet few. But when the number of his disciples began to increase by leaps and bounds, when he was
confessing crowds every morning, he was looked upon as
an abettor of Cacciaguerra. The more people that were confessed, the more went to Holy Communion. Hitherto Cacciaguerra's following had consisted almost solely of women,
who pressed to the altar-rail, row after row. That could be
pardoned, for women were notoriously devout. What excited sardonic comment was that the women were now
being joined at Communion by Philip's young men. This
was something unheard of. There were many people who
looked on it as being unhealthy, if not of dubious orthodoxy.
It was being called ostentatious and even hypocritical.

We must remember that though the Council of Trent
had pronounced in favor of frequent Communion, no definition had been given as to what was frequency. To go once

a month had been regarded as a sign either of extreme
sanctity or of disgusting affectation. And Cacciaguerra's
idea of frequent Communion was daily Communion. This,
his critics said, was being worse than a Theatine, and to
call a man a Theatine in those days was much the same
as to call him a Pharisee. Of course, everybody was a Christian; everybody hoped to get to heaven; but hardly anybody
considered that this sort of thing was necessary.

Cacciaguerra was not greatly liked. He had indeed his
devoted following, and it may be that his following admired him all the more because his severe face was marked,
as his biographer, Lady Amabel Kerr, puts it, "with the
scars of sin and repentance." Those who did not belong to
his following, however, thought that he was repulsive in
appearance. His remarkable personal history thrilled his
disciples when they heard it, but some of the other priests
at San Girolamo, who had nothing but commonplaces to
relate of themselves and who were decidedly not interesting, probably sometimes hinted that Cacciaguerra touched
up his romantic yarns. Apart from that, this man was a
standing rebuke to them. Like the majority of priests in
those days, they said Mass on Sundays but certainly not
every day during the week. Cacciaguerra by inducing his
lay disciples to receive Communion every day was felt to
be hitting at the clergy. His special apostolate therefore
was eyed somewhat askance and was, in fact, so one-sided
as to leave itself open to a good deal of legitimate theological criticism.

Cacciaguerra, had he been alone at San Girolamo, could
have been tolerated. But Cacciaguerra was by no means
alone; for Persiano Rosa had founded his confraternity,
and other clerics there already had little circles around them.
As Ponnelle comments, "Among the zealous priests at San

Girolamo there was a kind of mania for forming pious associations which each one grouped round himself."[2] The priests who were not particularly zealous could not be expected to like it, and they could say with some plausibility that these activities interfered with the ordinary work of the house. One eccentric could be put up with, but two . . . !

Cacciaguerra, however, cannot be fairly blamed for everything that happened. Nor perhaps need we directly accuse the devil, though the early biographers, and even Cardinal Capecelatro, say that it was the devil who stirred up the persecution that Philip was about to suffer. The devil does not have to put himself to much trouble about such matters. Knowing men as he does, he knows that there are plenty of undiscerning people who can be counted upon to be irritated with anybody the least out of the ordinary or with anything that interferes with their own convenience. And we may surmise that Philip Neri was something of a trial if only because he was a puzzle.

In the first place, there was that extraordinary joviality of his. It may be that in the beginning it was misunderstood, or that those who had made up their minds to disapprove of Philip found here another reason for disapproval. Perhaps he was set down as an exponent of that type of jocular Christianity which can be very distressing. His jests, when appearing as pendants to Cacciaguerra's grim austerity, were all the more noticeable. Both the austerity and the jocularity, viewed at a certain angle, could seem a pose, especially as they combined for the same ends.

---

[2] Teseo Raspa, whom Philip had known in the Banchi, but who was now a priest at San Girolamo, was one of these. Another was Enrico Pietra, another of Philip's disciples, who occupied himself while there in the work of remodelling and revivifying the Congregation for Christian Doctrine. The interests of these men had little to do with the activities for which the Archconfraternity of Charity had been established at San Girolamo. And this was still more true of Philip.

We may also surmise that Philip was regarded as a bit troublesome. Here were these young men of his coming in at the small hours for confession and hanging around all day, and again at night. It is easy to believe that there were complaints on that score, as there were complaints even in his own Congregation, when he founded it, that the youths in his room made a great deal of noise. The tramping up and down the stairs at all hours, the animated conversation, the peals of laughter — these things disturbed the monastic peace of San Girolamo.

It is clear that Philip particularly annoyed the two clerics who served as sacristans. Though, as it turned out, they were not all they should have been — for they were monks who had left the cloister without permission and so, in technical language, were "apostates" — they may nevertheless be entitled to a certain amount of our sympathy. They were inconvenienced by the fact that Philip always said his Mass at the unusual hour of noon. And when he did say it, he was inclined to be fussy about the vestments he wore, for he had a horror of anything in the least soiled. Worst of all, he showed a positive phobia against using a chalice that anybody else used, his fastidiousness being such, as we have seen, that he could not bring himself to drink out of a common glass. And though this was something that he set himself to conquer, it was at this time very strong in him. Moreover, the sacristans observed that the chalices they did give him were returned with the marks of his teeth actually showing at the rim, where he bit in the fierceness of his devotion. Orderly men, careful of the church property, could not be expected to like it. And if they were malicious men — as they seem to have been — they had in these things a convenient handle against Philip.

His way of saying Mass was itself an offence to them.

That he and Cacciaguerra should weep and sigh at the altar struck them as a hypocritical exhibition. They were not disposed to make any allowance for Philip's efforts to conceal his emotion by putting off his Mass to an hour when there would be hardly anybody in the church, or for his ordering the server to kneel in a place where his own face could not be seen or his transports noticed. The truth is that he said it as quickly as possible for fear that he might be carried away by an ecstasy. When elevating the Host he had to lower his arms instantly, or he might not get them down at all. It was beyond concealment that he was trembling the whole time, that when pouring the wine into the chalice he had to lean on the altar to steady himself, and that, when giving Communion, he sometimes seemed to be in danger of dropping the Hosts. That the sacristans — and other people as well — had some grounds for saying that this occasioned talk is comprehensible enough.

These two men found allies among other priests in the house, and a still more powerful ally in Vincenzo Teccosi, a doctor who was one of the deputies who governed the place and who probably was the medical officer of the Archconfraternity. As they were hardly in a position to tell Philip to get out, now that he had been assigned quarters there, and as he had refused the salary that would have made him amenable to the committee's jurisdiction, they adopted what is a common device in such cases and made up their minds to make life so unpleasant for him that he would be glad to withdraw of his own accord.

Discovering that he had an almost pathological dislike of old and soiled vestments, the sacristans always laid out for him the dirtiest they could find. Or when, rapt in his devotion, he was on his way to one altar they would go to him, just as he was about to begin, and send him to another.

They even went so far as to lock the sacristy door when he went to vest for Mass; they could always explain that he was so late that they thought he was not coming. There were many petty ways for making him miserable. They are not for a moment to be defended, but at least it can be understood how small-minded men who thought only of conventions were disturbed by Philip's habit of behaving as though he were a law unto himself.

Even his meals were taken in a Philippine style. He never ate as the other priests did in the refectory or his room. After Mass his server spread a napkin for him in the sacristy and gave him a couple of rolls and a tiny flask of wine. It was the only food he had all day. If he was given any meat, he distributed it among the altar-boys. That also struck them as a parade of austerity. "Theatine!" they snarled at him under their breath.

If the devil really had any hand in the acts of Dr. Teccosi and the sacristans, it is only one more proof that the devil is an ass. The sole result was an increase in Philip's patience and therefore in his sanctity. Once during Mass he fixed his eyes on the Crucifix above the altar and prayed: "O good Jesus, why is it that Thou dost not hear me? See how long a time I have besought Thee to give me patience! Why is it that Thou hast not heard me, and why is my soul disquieted with thoughts of anger and impatience?" The answer came, as though heard in the depths of his soul, "Dost thou not ask patience of Me, Philip? Behold I will give it thee speedily on this condition, that, if thy heart desire it, thou earn it through these temptations of thine." It was in this way that he learned to suffer fools — and in particular these officious fools — gladly.

The episodes described must have been extremely painful to one of his acute sensitiveness. Cacciaguerra, at whom the

persecution was primarily directed, was able to encase himself in the armor of his stern and imperious temperament.
Philip had no such defence. After Mass he was often so
exhausted that he had to go at once to his room and throw
himself on his bed. His sole way of escape was that he was
usually so completely wrapped in his dream that, as he
came from the altar, he saw nobody. If then he could pass
his closest friends without recognising them, he was still
more oblivious of the two spiteful sacristans and Dr. Teccosi. When he got upstairs he could retire to that *loggia*
he had built over his apartment — it was a kind of little
observatory or belvedere — and there pray with his eyes
over the panorama of Rome. It was always in such lofty
places that his heart went free. There he was safe; nobody
could trouble him there.

But even there he was always accessible to his disciples.
That was part of the complaints brought against him. Teccosi did not relish the idea of people coming in at all hours
of the day and night, yet Philip let them come, however
much they might interrupt him. There, too, he was often
in his dream. Fabrizio de' Massimi, having let himself into
the outer room by the key under the door, saw Philip standing with his eyes fixed on heaven and gesticulating not
only with his hands but his feet. For a full five minutes he
watched him, and Philip never saw that there was anyone
there, though his eyes were turned in Fabrizio's direction.
Not until Massimi spoke to him did Philip come to himself.
Then emerging from a daze he asked, "How did you get in?"

He had the same abstraction—only more intensely—when
he was saying Mass. He so frequently got absorbed that he
had to be prompted by the server, who pulled his chasuble
gently to remind him what to do next. Or he had to do
something utterly disconnected with the rubrics to bring

himself down to earth sufficiently to continue. Then he would walk the length of the altar several times, or turn to the server or make some remark about the lights. "Send away those dogs!" he would say; "Get rid of those beggars!" Anything would do that sounded plausible. There were times when, even to get himself into a state to say Mass at all, he had to read a few amusing pages from Mainardi's *Facezie*. Then his sense of humor would abate his over-powering sense of God sufficiently to enable him to get through the external actions and the words of the Holy Sacrifice.

Bacci says that Philip's bad treatment at the hands of Dr. Teccosi and the sacristans continued for about two years — that is, from 1552 to 1554. Actually it appears to have gone on rather longer and not to have ended completely until 1558, when the Cardinal Protector of the Archconfraternity took a hand in the affair and, so as to end the disturbances, appointed Cacciaguerra superior of the house. Bacci's ac-count makes what happened rather more dramatic than that. According to him, one of the sacristans, meeting Philip in the cloister, started to insult him. At this the other sacristan, who was by now feeling some compunction, came up and got into a fight with the man who had been associated with him in the persecution. Philip had to come to his rescue. The upshot was that both asked his pardon and, their con-sciences now touched, returned contritely to the monasteries they had deserted.[3] And Teccosi was also conquered at last by Philip's serene good humor and humility; kneeling

---

[3] If their contrition occurred in 1558, it may well have been prompted by terror. For, in the summer of that year, Paul IV proceeded with the utmost severity against the run-away monks in Rome, arresting over 200 of them. Some were even sentenced to the galleys. If an earlier date has to be found for the "apostates'" reconciliation with Philip, the men may still have been actuated by what was known to be coming.

down he asked forgiveness. One suspects, however, that the intervention of the Cardinal-Protector had a good deal to do with the matter. The important thing is that, in whatever way it happened, the storm at last blew itself out. Philip was left to pursue his course undisturbed.

By now his apartment had become too small to contain the men who gathered there. He was obliged to hold his conferences with the door open between his two rooms, but after a while the two together were insufficient for those who came. By 1554 or at latest 1555, the group migrated to an attic over the church to hold their meetings. It was an unpretentious enough place, and has been described as the granary and also as a passage leading to the organ; in neither event could it have been either comfortable or attractive. Nor could the use of this makeshift have been other than temporary; for though Philip and his disciples were tolerated there, they were not given formal permission to take this attic over for their use.

Yet Philip's Oratory by now was becoming the fashion. It was, however, still mainly attended by undistinguished men, many of them very poor and quite unlettered. Among these was a cobbler of the name of Stefano, an ex-soldier of a choleric and malicious temper. The first day he went, he took a back seat until Philip — whose habit it was to wander about, so as to make the acquaintance of newcomers — saw him and led him up to the front. His way of singling people out was often very effective. This time his kindly manner so captivated Stefano as to prepare the way for his conversion. He became notable for his obedience and his assiduity in prayer; for the next twenty-three years he was Philip's disciple. And what a change there was in him! Once when praying in the church of the Santissima Trinità di Ponte he was seen to be suddenly surrounded in resplendent light; always he was seen to be gentle and humble. The cantankerous old soldier had become a saint.

Of a similar type was another poor man named Francesco Maria, and commonly known as il Ferrarese. He earned his living as a vendor of clay images. Such was the purity and simplicity of life that developed in him, that he sometimes heard the angels sing, and he was notable for his gift of tears. On one occasion another Francesco Maria — the distinguished Tarugi — saw him standing lost in prayer and every now and then drawing back a pace or two, making gestures of astonishment. When Tarugi asked him why he did so, the answer came: "I am considering the greatness of God, and the more I consider it, the more it seems to grow before me, and its very immensity forces me to step backwards."

Then there was the Sicilian Tomaso. The height of his ambition was to become a sweeper of the floor at St. Peter's. There he stayed all day, except when he went to see Philip; there, too, he slept on the altar steps. One night the devil appeared to him in the form of a Negro. Tomaso immediately went up to the apparition and raised his fist for a blow. At this the devil vanished and Tomaso went back to his place as though nothing had happened and slept the night quietly through.

It is important to remember these men, because Philip never wanted the Oratory to be confined to fine gentlemen. They might come; when they did they were welcome. Not unnaturally, as time went on, Philip was to find his most active supporters, and afterwards the members of his Congregation, in such circles. But no social distinctions were ever permitted at the Oratory. If we hear more about the distinguished men than of those just mentioned, this was because they inevitably played the leading roles. The Oratory, however, was not intended to work solely among the elite.

But before mentioning some of the famous people who frequented it, Prospero Crivelli should come in, the cashier of the Cavalcanti bank whom Philip had converted when he was still a layman. In 1554 he thought he was dying and sent word to Philip. When Philip arrived, his friend reproached him, saying, "Why have you not come for two whole days? My doctor told me that I would die if my fever returned, and it *is* returning." Philip answered that he had stayed away because he had heard that Crivelli had made him his sole heir. "*I* your heir!" he exclaimed. "I do not want your legacy; leave it to somebody else. To show you that I don't want it, I am going to St. Peter's to pray for your recovery. If God won't give it in any other way, I shall offer Him my life for yours." When Philip talked in this style, people could be perfectly certain that he was going to get his prayers answered. There were times when, instead of asking God for something, he demanded it instead — and always seemed to obtain it. By the time he was back from St. Peter's Crivelli was perfectly healed.

It is possible that it was through Crivelli that Philip got acquainted with Giambattista Salviati, the brother of Antonio Maria Salviati, who became a cardinal. He was a cousin of Catherine de' Medici, the Queen of France, and a grand-nephew of Leo X — a very great personage indeed. However, Philip had had his wife, Porzia de' Massimi, as his penitent before winning her husband. She was one of the very few women we hear of at this time, for he did not encourage them to come to his confessional, his work being intended for men. When he got hold of the magnificent Giambattista, he specially picked him for such tasks as were likely to be most mortifying to him. He was not to be allowed to think that he was to do nothing but pray. While he was actually kneeling before the Blessed Sacrament he would feel his rich mantle being taken off and an infirmarian's apron being slipped around his neck instead. It was Philip's hint that it was time for him to go to the hospital.

In the Ospedale della Consolazione, Salviati one day found a former servant of his whom he asked to get up for a few minutes so that he might make his bed. The man supposed that he was being made game of, for he knew nothing about the change in his master's life. When at last he was brought to see that the grand Giambattista was really serious, he still was reluctant to allow the cousin of the Queen of France to perform so menial a service. But in the end the bed was made by the master for the man.

Salviati was one of those Philip selected as a favorite victim. He was always being told to do something humiliating or absurd, and he always obeyed, even when he was ordered to sweep a church porch or to carry Philip's dog through the streets. On the other hand, when, of his own accord, he dismissed his retinue and began to dress very simply, Philip said he was wrong. He was to keep the attendants his rank demanded; and while his clothes might be plain, they were to be appropriate for his station. Even in what appeared to be his eccentricities Philip always showed a great deal of common-sense.

Another splendid gentleman who was obliged to carry Philip's dog — and who wrote a humorously querulous sonnet on what he suffered in doing so — was Francesco Maria Tarugi. He had started out as a soldier, but, when his uncle, Julius III, was elected Pope, he thought he saw the chance of more rapid advancement in the Church. If he declined the offered bishopric, it was with an eye on the cardinalate.

But Julius died and his successor, Marcellus II — another uncle of Tarugi's — reigned only three weeks; so again he was thinking of a military career when Cardinal Farnese took him into his household. It was then that he met Philip, and the whole course of his life was altered. He was induced to make an hour of mental prayer, and in this he experienced such spiritual sweetness that he kept coming back. "From that moment," he was to say, "I felt burning within me a bright flame, which my sins could not extinguish, and which never ceased to torment me until the time when I gave myself entirely into his hands." If he held back a month, this was because of a love affair. But the lady died and he became a priest and the most famous preacher of his time. The Oratory never had a more brilliant recruit, though possibly Baronius was a still greater man than the one upon whom he conferred the title of *Dux verbi*. He was made a cardinal archbishop, but at the end resigned all his titles and when past eighty became a simple Oratorian Father again.

A less notable man than Tarugi, but one almost his equal in social position, was Costanzo Tassone, the nephew of Cardinal Bertani and the majordomo of Cardinal Santa Fiora. His conversion, occurring at the same time as that of Salviati and Tarugi, caused an immense sensation in Rome. Like Tarugi, he entered the priesthood but was of a rather restless disposition. When St. Charles kept begging Philip to let him have some men for his diocese of Milan, Philip let Tassone go — regarding him as an able man but one whom he was willing to spare. Santa Fiora did not at all like it when Philip lured his majordomo away, and as it was Tassone who first led the Cardinal's dog, Capriccio, to Philip's room — with the result that the animal would never go back to his former master — there was a further grumble,

"He is not content with taking men from me, but takes away even my animals!" It was that celebrated beast that was made such use of in providing unusual mortifications for the splendidly dressed gentlemen who had to carry him through the jeering streets.

Chapter Six

ORATORY AND ORATORIO

THOUGH 1558 is the "official" date for the beginning of the Oratory, it is certain that the attic of the church of San Girolamo, which was to be its first meeting-place, had been in use at least since 1555. Probably the later date indicates no more than that permanent possession was then taken of the room; until that time Philip and his disciples had been there on sufferance. The new arrangement may have been introduced because in 1558 Cacciaguerra was made superior of San Girolamo and Dr. Teccosi won over to be Philip's friend. Even so, the Oratory was fitted up at Philip's expense, though by this time he could of course draw freely upon the wealth of some of his new disciples.

The larger meeting place was necessary because of the number of men who now attended.[1] And as there were so many of them the old informal way of conducting the conferences was no longer feasible. Small intimate groups still met as before in Philip's room, but for the main gathering a definite mode of procedure was necessary. Yet the conversational tone was retained and all the speakers sat as they spoke, though by degrees the little platform on which they

---

[1] The room, however, did not have seating space for more than a hundred. It could, presumably, have held another hundred who stood. For some years it was, no doubt, more than large enough.

sat was raised higher above the floor and the addresses themselves were prepared instead of being improvised on the spur of the moment. It was at this time, too, that there began to be a musical program at the end of every session. That, like the other new departures, was of the utmost importance.

It was just at this moment, however, that Philip came near to throwing up his work in Rome and starting something entirely new. It could hardly have been due to the opposition he was experiencing, for by this time that opposition had considerably lessened, if it had not entirely ceased. The fact that Philip entertained the idea of a new venture must be set down to his impulsive and generous nature; but that he eventually refrained was due to his good sense. Never after this was there to be the slightest doubt in his mind as to where his true work lay.

In 1552 Francis Xavier, who had been Philip's friend, died deserted except by a young Chinese on the island of Sancian off the coast of a China that proved impenetrable. But St. Francis' wonderful letters had been published, and they were read aloud in the Oratory, where they deeply stirred everybody. Over and over again in those letters there were appeals for helpers. It was impossible for the heart not to be moved by a passage like this: "How many there are . . . who are thinking only of getting a high position in the Church through their reputation for learning, instead of using their acquirements for the common good. If only they would leave their miserable ambitions and say, 'Lord, here am I. Send me wherever Thou wilt — even to India!' how much better their own state would be when they come to die." Philip and his enthusiastic friends in their attic did not take such things merely as edifying passages; they thought they should act. Twenty of them — among them two doctors named Modio and Fucci, about whom we shall hear more later — made plans to go out to the Orient as missionaries. Several of these men were even ordained priests in readiness for just such a step. It was one more manifestation of the Xaverian flame then sweeping the world.

Yet perhaps we should not set this project down solely to missionary zeal. For though the opposition to Philip was dying down at San Girolamo, new difficulties of an even more serious sort threatened. The pontificate of Julius III (1550–1555) had been one of partial reaction, following the reforms initiated by Paul III. That the old laissez-faire spirit had to some extent returned had given Philip his chance; official indifference had left him free to follow his own unconventional devices. But with the election of Paul IV a drastic change at once occurred.[2] The new pope was described by the Florentine ambassador as "a man of iron, and the very stones over which he walks emit sparks which cause a conflagration should his wishes not be carried out." He made himself an object of dread, lecturing his cardinals as though they were a set of idle schoolboys, imprisoning or exiling several, and threatening them all. While it must be admitted that the tall, thin, irascible old fighter Carafa accomplished a good deal, he often defeated his own purposes by his violence. And Philip, while he welcomed reform, must have been dubious about the Pope's high-handed methods. Capecelatro suggests that these — and in particular his mixing a reform policy in the Church with his efforts to eject Spain from Italy — account, at least in part, for

---

[2] The reign of Marcellus II would have been equally one of reform, but of reform carried out by milder means. But this pope from whom so much had been expected died twenty-two days after his election, leaving the door open for a reformer of a very different type.

Philip's feeling disheartened, especially as the Pope's secular policies were so largely inspired by his ambitious and unworthy nephew, Cardinal Carlo Carafa. Ponnelle may be correct in saying that: "With the accession of Paul IV, Philip became, in contrast with him, the man of the moment; he became so by reason of his lovable character, in proportion as the Pope showed himself intolerant and severe. He was the very man to free the reform to which men of all sorts had to submit, whether they liked it or not, from its repellent aspects and to make it attractive." This, however, is a judgment reached in retrospect; it was by no means obvious at the time. Philip's position was anything but secure, and he may well have felt that he could do his work in Rome only if he was allowed to do it in his own way. It is very likely that he had reason to fear that his Oratory might fall under the suspicion of the harsh reformer seated on the papal throne.

Be this as it may, there can be no doubt that he was strongly attracted by the idea of going to India for its own sake. The amazing fact is that where Francis Xavier, with the highly organized Society of Jesus behind him, could secure recruits only by twos and threes, Philip immediately contrived to secure twenty enthusiastic volunteers. How his project was to be financed does not appear, for though the prospective missionaries no doubt were quite prepared to live in absolute poverty on their arrival, it would still have been a costly undertaking to get them there at all. Presumably Philip was counting on the rich friends he had made during the past year or two; he must have had enough foresight to have considered ways and means. There is no indication at all that he intended to affiliate himself and his disciples with either the Jesuits or the Franciscans who were already in India.

He had enough prudence not to rush into such a scheme without prayer and seeking advice. The advice he sought from a Benedictine monk who lived at St. Paul's, and the monk — who was at a loss what to say — referred him to a Cistercian named Vincenzo Ghettini, the prior of the monastery at the Tre Fontane. The wizened little man of eighty with the great dark eyes was reputed to have visions of St. John the Evangelist.

To this Cistercian Philip unfolded his project and was told to come back later for an answer. When he did so, the monk said something in which true and false prophecies were mingled. The false part of the prophecy was that he had seen the Three Fountains flowing with blood. Since 1527 there were people who had never ceased predicting a second sack of Rome, one that never occurred. And this part of his answer Agostino must have drawn out of his inner consciousness; it was taken as implying that, if Philip would only stay where he was, he would have all the martyrdom for which he thirsted. That St. John, however, had duly appeared and had said that Philip's Indies were to be in Rome was far more likely. That part of the prophecy was abundantly fulfilled. It was accepted as decisive and ended once and for all every thought of foreign missionary work. With complete peace of mind Philip therefore went on with what he was doing.

His was always a day by day improvisation. Never did he form plans for the future. The Oratory — that is, the Oratory considered as the meetings of his young men — was still only in process of development. There was no hard-and-fast procedure; spontaneity remained its special charm, and though circumstances were making it necessary to introduce by degrees a greater amount of system, Philip was always delighted whenever it was possible to revert to the former style of simply reading a few pages from a book and making or inviting comments. Even when set addresses became the general rule, anything like rhetorical language was discouraged in favor of conversational simplicity; and this was further emphasised by the fact that those who spoke did so sitting down. It was still talk rather than preaching. If anybody attempted to show off his eloquence, even if anybody dealt with abstract instead of practical subjects, Philip would instantly stop him.

Baronius, the great historian — a historian in spite of himself and only because he was under orders from Philip — gave in the eighth volume of his *Annals,* published just after Philip's death, an account of the meetings at the Oratory as they were in the years subsequent to the time that he first attended them in 1557. The passage is worth quoting in its entirety. Commenting on the assemblies of the primitive Christians, he affirmed that there was a revival of their spirit and even of their form at the Oratory, when he wrote: "It is certainly by the divine disposition that we have seen, in great part, renewed in our day in the city of Rome what the Apostle commanded to be done for the profit of the Church, in the method of discoursing of the things of God to the edification of the hearers. This has been the work of the Reverend Father Philip Neri of Florence, who like a skillful architect laid the foundations of it, and of the Reverend Father Francesco Maria Tarugi of Montepulciano, his scholar, who for the excellence of his preaching might well be called the captain of the Word of God. To the pains and industry of these two was primarily owing the arrangement that every day those who were desirous of Christian perfection should come to the Oratory of San Girolamo, from which the Congregation of the Oratory afterwards took its name, and there hold a pious and devout meeting in the fol-

lowing manner: after some time spent in mental prayer, one
of the brothers read a spiritual book, and in the middle of
the reading, the Father who superintended the whole discoursed upon what was read, explaining it with greater accuracy, enlarging upon it, and insinuating it into the hearts
of the readers. Sometimes he desired one of the brothers
to give his opinion on the subject, and then the discourse
proceeded in the form of a dialogue; and this exercise lasted
one hour, to the great consolation of the audience. After
this, one of his own people, at his command, mounted to a
seat raised a few steps above the rest, and without any
adornment of language discoursed upon some approved lives
of the saints, illustrating what he said by passages of Scripture or sentences of the Fathers. He was succeeded by another, in the same style, but on a different subject; and lastly
came a third, who discoursed upon ecclesiastical history.
Each of them was allowed only half an hour. When all this
was finished, to the wonderful contentment as well as profit
of the hearers, they sang some spiritual canticle, prayed
again for a short time, and so the exercise finished. . . . It
seemed as though the ancient apostolical and beautiful
method of Christian assemblies was renewed."

Baronius in his modesty does not tell us that it was he
who delivered these discourses on ecclesiastical history,
or that when he began he was just over twenty and a layman. Others of the regular speakers in those early days were
also laymen. One of these, Tarugi, was to die, like Baronius
himself, a cardinal. Another, the brilliant Giovan Francesco
Bordini, was to become a bishop. But others, like the two
doctors Antonio Fucci and Giambattista Modio — both of
whom had volunteered to go with Philip to India — were
to remain laymen to the end. The Oratory in its inception
was essentially a lay apostolate. Philip could not forget

the work he had done as a layman in Rome for nearly eighteen years.

Modio deserves more than passing mention. Shortly before falling in with Philip — that is, in 1554 — he had published his *Convitto,* a humorous book but one that was far from edifying. Had he attempted to bring it out when Paul IV was pope, it would assuredly have been prohibited. But of course by that time Modio would not have wished to have published anything of the kind; by then he was the Oratory's most acceptable speaker on the lives of the saints. Ponnelle makes the excuse — though not specially for Modio — that in this age the scabrous was considered witty in itself and that those who adopted such a mode of being funny were merely following a convention that did not necessarily indicate anything reprehensible in their personal lives. This may be true; all the same, Modio's *Convitto* would not have been written had he met Philip before composing it. His later literary work was of a very different sort. It was a commentary on the *laudi* of Jacopone da Todi — a sign of his complete conversion.

The account Baronius has left of these early meetings makes only casual reference to the music with which the three-hour sessions concluded. Probably not all those who attended remained for the whole time. Doubtless people were coming and going, so that the end of each half hour may have been a signal for departures, consequently also for the late arrivals, standing at the back, to take the vacated seats. But it would seem that the more fervent of the group stayed the whole afternoon and that for these some diversion was considered necessary. It was for this reason that there was music.

What it is important to note is that this music was provided by the very best musicians in Rome and that it served to attract men to the Oratory who would not have gone otherwise. But while being a relaxation after the strain of listening to a number of addresses, it was also used to supplement those addresses by augmenting fervor in another way. Finally it should be remarked that out of this music developed the musical form of the oratorio, whose very name reveals that it was derived from Philip's Oratory. Therefore, Philip had not a little to do with the history of music.

With his poetic and artistic nature, Philip had a natural affinity with musicians. Among his earliest penitents at San Girolamo were Delia Buscaglia, who was married to the well-known instrumentalist Gaspare Brissio and whose son was the composer Giovanni Francesco Brissio. Another was Bradamante Pacelli, whose husband was to be choirmaster at the court of King Sigismund III of Poland and whose sister, Fulvia, was the mother of the composer Giovanni Francesco Anerio. Still another was Sebastiano, who was in charge of the music at the Castle of Sant' Angelo. On his death-bed he was consoled by Philip, just as it was Philip who effected a miraculous cure for Bradamante Pacelli.

The name of Sebastiano leads to others still more celebrated — those of Giovanni Animuccia and Pier Luigi da Palestrina, the one the choirmaster at the Lateran and the other at St. Peter's. They, like all the musicians who attended, gave their services for nothing. Not only that; they made many special compositions for the Oratory, both for the hymns sung there and (what is of greater importance, so far as musical history is concerned) for the dramatic recitatives from the Bible that seem first to have been given at these exercises. This variety of musical composition, which in the eighteenth and nineteenth centuries was to receive a very wide application and to become immensely popular, did not have, it is true, a full development at the Oratory;

but it was there nevertheless that the possibilities of the pattern were first recognised. Here, at least in germ, was oratorio — a combination of the lyric and the epic, just as opera is a combination of the lyric and the play, both being in their origin very Italian. No doubt the connection with the Oratory was something of an accident — Philip's happening to fall in with musicians, and in particular with Animuccia — but had that accident not occurred, the oratorio might never have come into being at all.

It goes without saying of course that Philip did not have in mind the creation of a new musical form. All he was thinking of was something appropriate for the close of his meetings; and there were at hand men who could give him just what he wanted, a novelty for which his young men felt it was well worth waiting through three hours of talk. Here many of the *laudi* of Jacopone da Todi were well adapted to a combination of solos and the responses of a choir. This might be illustrated from the opening of one of the *laudi*, as translated by Mrs. Theodore Beck, given in Miss Underhill's book. The Soul and the Angels must be understood to alternate in these stanzas:

> Teach me and lead me on
>   To find my love so sweet;
> No longer would I grieve my Lord
>   By pause, or by retreat:
> Sore hath He mourned the tarrying of my feet,
>   Hath waited long for me.
>
> If thou wouldst find thy Love,
>   Christ Jesus, sweet and fair,
> Behold, Humility's dark vale!
>   Thou needst must enter there:
> Many have breathed that Valley's heavy air; —
>   We tell thee faithfully.

O counsel me, I pray!
  My heart is sore be-stead;
Show me the path, that steadfastly
  Right onward I may tread:
That I may hold my way, nor turn my head,
  Nor stray confusedly.

Humility's dark path
  Hath but a narrow gate;
Yet, entered there, thy journey lies
  More easy and more straight:
Thou shalt find consolation in that state,
  Yea, comfort fair and free.

Even in a somewhat labored translation it will be at once
seen how that lends itself to part-singing. And the sentiments were precisely those Philip most wished to inculcate.
"From this," Ludwig von Pastor remarks, "it was but a single
step to the performance of those narratives and stories after
the manner of the later musical Oratorios."

This last step was taken by Giovanni Francesco Anerio,
himself one of Philip's young men. For his book of music,
published in 1619, twenty-four years after Philip's death,
another of the musical members of the Oratory group, the
papal singer Orazio Griffi, then very old, wrote the preface,
in which he describes the Oratorian exercises at which he
had assisted for forty-five years. Pastor in a long footnote
writes: "The point [made by Griffi] which has been over-
looked by the biographers of Philip, but which is of great
importance, runs as follows: 'There could not have been an
easier or more efficacious means of exciting souls to a perfect love and fear of God than those daily considerations
of the hatefulness of sin, of the punishments of hell, of the
beauty of holy souls, of eternal happiness; in this way hearts
were disposed to penance, urged to the frequent reception

of Holy Communion, and to the performance of works of charity. And this was your work, Blessed Philip. . . . In order to attain to your zealous ends and to attract sinners by means of sweet recreation to the holy exercises of the Oratory, you made use of music and caused sacred songs to be performed in common; in this way the people were allured by the singing and the sermons to the good of their souls. Some came to the Oratory only for the music, but then became more adaptable and sensible of the spiritual exhortations, and were converted to God with great fervor."

Philip was certainly fortunate in being able to supply his gatherings every day with music that was absolutely first-rate, and which was in itself so great an inducement to attendance. There came the composers, who often sang, playing their instruments at the same time, and singers from the chief church choirs, and such famous instrumentalists as the trumpeters Fabio de Amatis and Gaspare Brissio.

But of course the two most resplendent names are those of Animuccia and Palestrina. Pious as these men were, they might not have gone to the Oratory had it not been for the fact that musicians there were given a wider range than in any of the great basilicas, as these did not use vernacular motets and madrigals and *laudi*. Philip encouraged them to experiment, and they were glad of the opportunity he provided.

Animuccia first went to Philip in the year he succeeded Palestrina as choirmaster at St. Peter's, that is, in 1556. He published in 1563, 1565, and 1570 three collections of *laudi* compiled specially for the use of the Oratory. In the last of these he explained his purpose; it was that of producing richly harmonised compositions, "refraining, so far as I can, from the complications of fugues and other devices, so as not to obscure the sense of the words." His object was much

the same as that of the greater Palestrina himself — a combination of the highest musical beauty with the perfect
intelligibility of what was sung.

When Animuccia died in 1571 in Philip's arms, the direction of the music at the Oratory was taken over by Palestrina, who at the same time succeeded Animuccia at St.
Peter's. Though his best work was in his Masses, there can
be no doubt that his madrigals and motets, especially those
in praise of the Blessed Virgin, were often sung at the
meetings of the Oratory. It was to these that Philip alluded
when, on the Feast of the Purification, 1594, Philip found
Palestrina dying. "My son," he said to him, "would it not
gladden you to go and enjoy the feast which today is held
in heaven in honor of the Queen of angels and saints?" The
reply was, "Yes, I do most eagerly desire it. May Mary
obtain for me this grace from her divine Son." Though the
authenticity of that story has been questioned, it is certain
that Palestrina and Philip were on intimate terms and that
he had much to do with the musical performances at the
Oratory.

Mention finally should be made of Francisco Soto. Coming from Spain in 1560, he became one of the soprano
singers of the papal choir; and when in 1575 he joined the
Congregation of the Oratory and was ordained priest, he
still retained his connection with St. Peter's. But this doctor
of simplicity, as they called him, was not content with his
musical talents; he aspired to be a preacher as well. His
main use to the Oratory, however, was his music, in which
he was unlike Giovanni Severano, who joined Philip's community in 1589 and who, though he was an excellent mu-
sician, was still more distinguished as an archaeologist.

The presence of these musicians not only attracted people
to the Oratory exercises but had much to do with the prodi-

gious success of Philip's picnics. Yet to call them picnics is, of course, only a manner of speaking. They were really pilgrimages to which Philip very wisely gave a festive atmosphere. When they were started in 1553, it was only in a small way, with about thirty men in the party. The excursions had been organized that year because, under Julius III, the Carnival had been allowed to come back with much of its license. It was in order to keep his disciples away from amusements which Philip feared might be occasions of sin that he hit upon the idea of introducing them to his favorite devotion of visits to the Seven Churches. At the same time he believed that to have nothing but piety on these excursions would probably be to defeat his object. If they were to be a counter-attraction to the Carnival they had to be gay. They became so very popular that some years later — though by then there was no competing carnival — as many as two or three thousand people would go. These were of all classes, the vast majority being the laymen for whom they were intended but always with some priests among them, especially Capuchins and Dominicans. The only people not allowed to go on these outings were women.

The order of the day was a visit in turn to St. Peter's and St. Paul's, at each of which church Philip would preach a short sermon. This would be followed by Mass at San Sebastiano, when most of the company would receive Holy Communion. Then they would go to the vineyard of the Massimi or the Crescenzi where they would sit on the grass and eat a light breakfast of bread and cheese, with a hard-boiled egg and some fruit and a little wine. During this picnic repast the musicians would always play and the singers perform. But indeed the party never ceased singing from the moment they set out, for, as Bacci says, "they had musicians with them the whole way." After which delightful period of recreation they would go on to visit the rest of the Seven Churches.

So large a body of pilgrims had to be divided into companies, and Philip would pass from one to the other, his arrival always giving sparkle to the whole group. Many men went on these pilgrimages, as many went to the Oratory, only out of curiosity to hear laymen preach or to hear the singing and the trumpeters from Sant' Angelo. But the result was much the same as at the Oratory meetings. Though attendance did not guarantee conversion, it was never quite safe for anyone to go unless he was prepared to be converted.

One would have supposed that these excursions would have been considered very harmless, even if they did not have a spiritual purpose, even if they had not been intended, at any rate in the beginning, to provide a counter-attraction to the Carnival. But no; they got Philip a good deal of criticism. It must be remembered that he had hardly emerged from his troubles at San Girolamo and that a certain amount of suspicion still attached to him as an innovator. His very success at the Oratory incurred envy; and by allowing laymen to preach he was doing something that most people considered highly questionable. Now these spectacular picnics of his brought the charge that he was creating a political party, or a new religious sect — the charge varied with the accuser — and that he was, in either event, a dangerously ambitious man. In 1559 the Cardinal Vicar of Rome, Virgilio Rosario, sent for him and vented his tirade. "I am surprised," he said, "that you are not ashamed of yourself, you who affect to despise the world, and yet go about enticing numbers of people to follow you; and all to win favor with the multitude, and to work your way, under pretext of sanctity, to some prelacy or other!" He peremptorily withdrew for two weeks Philip's faculties for hearing confessions and ordered him not to go out accompanied by the crowds that always came at his heels.

The whole thing seems very absurd. Philip was to prove many times during his life that nobody could be seeking ecclesiastical promotion less than himself. But something else was at the back of Rosario's mind. He felt that all of Philip's activities needed investigation. Had it been merely a question of good-natured (or for that matter, malicious) jokes about the pious picnics, the whole thing could have been ignored. Such jokes were made. People chuckled and told one another that Philip had taken no less than seven mules laden with tarts. Cardinals asked how many cold chickens Father Philip had eaten that day. Meanwhile Rosario pondered more serious matters.

It should be borne in mind that, if the Cardinal Vicar acted as he did, it was more or less under the Pope's instructions. And there was some reason for this. The year 1559, which was to be the last of Paul IV's turbulent pontificate, was also the most tragic. Not only had his anti-Spanish policy failed; he had received the appalling blow of discovering that Cardinal Carlo Carafa, his nephew, and other relatives whom he had advanced to high positions, were thorough-going scoundrels. The whole gang, with the exception of Cardinal Alfonso Carafa, who was not implicated in their crimes, were ejected from Rome and the Pope never would see them again. His heart was broken at the thought that, in spite of his almost ferocious efforts at general reform, the worst scandals should have cropped up in his own family. During the next reign (that of Pius IV) Cardinal Carlo Carafa and others of his relatives were actually executed for their misdeeds. Paul IV was at least spared the blow of their murder of the Duchess of Paliano, for this occurred a few days after his death.

It is hardly matter of wonder that the temper of Paul IV, which was never one of the best, should have become still more sour and savage and suspicious. And Philip could not have increased his standing in official circles by his attitude to the condemnation of the writings of Savonarola. Some Jesuits and Augustinians had worked for their being put upon the Index, and might have succeeded had it not been for Cardinal Ghisleri (the future Pius V) and Ercolani, the prior of the Minerva. It was known also that Giambattista Salviati, Philip's disciple, had done all he could for the Dominicans and that the Dominicans themselves, in order to avert the threatened calamity, had gone in for devotions that Rosario considered "superstitious." Philip's part in all this probably accounts for the charge that he was creating a "party," something about which the Pope was exceedingly nervous in those days of his vast unpopularity. It should not be supposed, therefore, that Philip was being singled out; he was merely one of many who, Rosario thought, should be watched.

In the end more moderate counsels prevailed with regard to Savonarola. Yet it was for a time touch-and-go. Every day that passed without a condemnation was celebrated at the Minerva with a *Te Deum,* and when the final decision was reached the Dominicans, their firm partizan Philip among them, were kneeling in adoration before the Blessed Sacrament. It was then that Philip had one of the most celebrated of his ecstasies. When he came to, he exclaimed, "Victory, victory, my dear friends! The Lord has heard our prayer; victory, victory!" It turned out later that at that very hour it had been determined that the writings of Savonarola should not be placed upon the Index of Prohibited Books. Though a few of the friar's more violent sermons were proscribed — not so much because they were heretical as because it was wished that something be done to save the faces of those who had demanded an *in toto* condemnation — the Dominicans were able to feel that they had triumphed. And Rosario, who had worked against Savonarola, saw in Philip's action one more indication that he was not quite sound.

All these circumstances should be borne in mind when considering what is called Philip's "persecution." If they are borne in mind, Rosario's attitude toward Philip becomes understandable enough. There is no need to drag in the machinations of the devil.

The early biographers see in the sudden death of Rosario, shortly after he had suspended Philip's faculties, a sign of the judgment of God — and this though Philip pointed out that men do, after all, die quite suddenly from natural causes. Bacci even sees in the death of some of those who had made jokes about Philip's picnics another manifestation of the wrath of God, though one wonders how many of us would live long if heaven took all our jokes so seriously. To round out the melodrama we are given a story of a strange priest in a habit that was not recognised as that of any particular order — though the description of it would seem to point to a Franciscan — coming into a meeting at the Oratory with a revelation from God that they should have the Forty Hours' Devotion and that then the persecution would cease. After this, of course, he mysteriously departed, and Rosario mysteriously died.

What is certain is that Rosario's death did remove an enemy. The Pope now took a hand in the investigation and satisfied himself that there was nothing to reprehend in the exercises of the Oratory. So far from that, the people he appointed to look into the matter reported that in the preaching at San Girolamo there was a remarkable union of fervor and soundness. As soon as he heard this, Paul IV sent Philip, as a token of his approval, a couple of the painted candles from his own chapel — ones that had been lit the previous Candlemas Day — and word that he would like to attend the meetings at the Oratory did time permit.

But time was running out for Pope Paul IV. The trial to which Philip had been subjected occurred at Eastertide, 1559, a period specially devoted to Philip's pilgrimages. The Pope died on August 19 of the same year, weighed down with grief. He had been passionately sincere in his desire to effect reform, and perhaps his violent methods were necessary, conditions being what they were. But his severity had been at times tyrannical and even cruel, and as soon as it was known that he was dead, there was much unabashed rejoicing in Rome. The populace pulled down his statue on the Capitol, and threw its head into the Tiber. As for the arms of the Carafa family, they were destroyed wherever they were found.

As was to be expected, the election of his successor fell upon a moderate. Yet Pius IV did not react against the policies of Paul; it was only that he adopted different methods for achieving the same results — methods that in the long run turned out to be more effective than those of the fiery Giampietro Carafa. For the Oratory, as for the Church, the new pontificate was providential. In the new and more temperate atmosphere it could grow without apprehensions as to its future. In nothing was the new reign more fortunate than in the fact that Pius IV at once created his twenty-two-year-old nephew to be a Cardinal and Secretary of State and Archbishop of Milan — though he was still a layman. By so doing, he for once justified the nepotism that had so often proved itself odious. For Charles Borromeo was a saint; and he was to be the closest of Philip's friends.

Chapter Seven

THE MAKING OF A HISTORIAN

T HE chief feature of the Oratory, properly so called, was the afternoon meetings. But there were other activities which should at least be indicated. At the end of the three-hour sessions of informal addresses and delightful music, Philip would usually take for a walk as many of those who chose to go with him. After sitting still for so long, a stretching of the legs and some fresh air was desirable. And these little walks attracted a good deal of attention, especially as they were by no means made in demure silence. It was then that Philip was in his most vivacious and whimsical mood. Often enough the things he did and said made passers-by turn round and stare. As a rule they went to the Minerva to hear Vespers, but on the way back to San Girolamo there was more animated conversation and loud laughter again — and sometimes even what looked to be clowning, when Philip went out of his way to make himself or some beloved victim ridiculous in public. There is hardly matter for surprise that staid people disapproved or that Philip was delated to Rosario. Yet even during the brief period in 1559 when he was forbidden to go through the streets accompanied by his disciples, the disciples continued to follow him at a short distance — which itself excited remark.

On Sundays and feast days — people then being free from their usual occupations — those who were with Philip on these walks might number several hundreds. Then, if the weather was fine, they would go up the Janiculum Hill to the Church of Sant' Onofrio. It was in the monastery attached to it that Tasso spent the last month of his life, and under an old tree beside it the Roman municipality put up in 1898 the following inscription: "In the shade of this oak, Torquato Tasso, when the laurels he had sighed for were close at hand, but death likewise, brooded silently over his unhappy life, and Philip Neri amid the happy shouts of boys became a boy himself again — most wisely."

There in the meadow the company would play ball or piastrella. And Philip always took a hand in the beginning. But as soon as the sports had got well underway, he had a habit of retiring to a slight elevation, where he would draw from his pocket a little book containing the last chapters of the four Gospels, those giving an account of the Passion. In tears he would meditate, until some bright-eyed boy ran up to him begging him to come and join them again, which he always did. In playing with them he knew that he was serving God.

On special occasions, instead of holding the meetings in the usual place, Philip would take his disciples to this or some other outdoor place and hold a kind of "gala" oratory. We hear of as many as three or four thousand people attending in 1578, and women were permitted to go. Instead of the customary discourses a boy would preach a sermon he had learned by heart, as a charming and playful substitute. Edification would be obtained, but not less effectively because it was given in this way; and there would be more music than ever.

This sort of thing served as a baiting of the hook for the

smaller gatherings that were held indoors and that were strictly limited to men. In addition to the afternoon exercises there were meetings for prayer every evening, and these had a definite form. There was meditation in silence for half an hour, after which there was another half hour of vocal prayers — recitation of the litanies and the like. And shocking as this may sound in modern ears, three times a week the whole assembly took the discipline in common.

To soothe those who may be disturbed to hear of this manifestation of medieval asceticism, it might be added that this scourging could hardly have been particularly gory. The purpose was the inculcation of humility rather than the infliction of bodily pain. But Philip did not wish his followers to get the idea that the spiritual life was all music and picnics. Though he was no great advocate of external mortifications — "If you wish to go to extremes," he was to write in 1578, "let it be in sweetness, patience, humility and charity" — he did not by any means refuse them all value. While the mortifications he normally imposed on his disciples were of a different sort — and sometimes were rather quaint or comical, such as were intended to destroy their self-esteem — the taking of the discipline remained a regular procedure among his young men. Perhaps it was all the more necessary because he had many very talented men around him — Modio and Fucci, the two physicians who discoursed so eloquently on the lives of the saints, and Animuccia and Palestrina, the great composers, and the brilliant Tarugi and Bordini, and finally Cesare Baronius, who was destined to be the father of church history.

Of all this group surely the grandest figure was that of Baronius. He may not have had the obviously glittering talents of Bordini and Tarugi, yet the work he accomplished had a more enduring value than anything they did. And under his somewhat lumpish and phlegmatic exterior there was a dog-like fidelity which still touches all those who hear of it.

He had arrived in Rome in 1557 from his native Abruzzi with the hope of getting taken into the household of a cardinal. Instead he fell in with Philip, and though he had no serious sins of which to repent — the worst being an evening of revelry in a tavern — it was in the Oratory that his spiritual life was developed. It was to Philip also that he owed the job he obtained — that of tutor to Ottavio Paravicini, the future cardinal.

Like other young laymen, he was called upon to make his discourses in the attic room. And Philip was amused with the way the "barbarian," as he called him, began with the most portentous gravity to expatiate on the horrors of hell and the enormity of sin. Though Baronius was not without a sense of humor, it seemed to evaporate the moment he took the speaker's chair to deliver one of his blood-curdling discourses.

It may have been merely to divert him from such subjects that Philip assigned to Baronius the daily address on church history. But whether or not that was his object, he soon came to perceive that it was in this field that the true gifts of Baronius lay. So grumble as Baronius might, Philip insisted that he stick to history.

Those who spoke at the meetings were encouraged to do so without premeditation and according to the inspiration of the moment. It is, of course, obvious that history is not to be dealt with in this fashion. To talk or write about it, a man must study it; and Baronius, in his plodding, dogged way, was so very thorough in his researches, even from the outset, that it was clear that he had the special temperament

for such work. It may have been just a lucky accident that
Philip picked him; perhaps it was merely to see what he
could do. But even if there was no great insight at the beginning, certainly a very keen insight recognised that
Baronius could be developed into a very great historian
— an insight all the more remarkable because Philip himself
had nothing of the historian's make-up.

Baronius did not have an idea at the outset to what stu-
pendous task he was being led. Nor, for that matter, did
Philip; this was something that dawned on him by degrees,
though Baronius came to credit him with having known
from the start that the *Annals* were to be the ultimate outcome of his little lectures. Baronius, of course, should know,
and he was perfectly correct in saying that his discourses
were "a trial of strength." They were so in effect; as to
whether they were so in intention is questionable. What is
certain is that even when Philip came to see of what his
disciple was capable, he would not allow him to spoil his
undertaking by haste. Only after Baronius had covered the
entire ground seven times, taking thirty years to do so, did
Philip set him to writing his monumental work. Not until
then did Philip consider that he was adequately prepared.

We know all this from Baronius himself, because in the
preface to the eighth massive volume of the *Annals,* which
was published after Philip's death, with four more volumes
to follow, he inserted as dedication what he called "A
Thanksgiving to the Blessed Philip Neri." In it he says,
among other things, "I set myself . . . to this great undertaking, after repeated orders from him, very much against
my own will, objecting and entirely distrusting my ability
for such a work. I undertook it out of obedience to the will
of God, and on this ground also he constantly urged me for-

ward whenever, overpowered by my burden, I interrupted the work for a short time, and with sharp rebukes compelled me to return to my task immediately."

But having said this, Baronius makes, very gently, a kind of complaint. Though Philip would not allow him to turn a hair's breadth from the *Annals,* he expected him to perform all his other duties as well. "Often, I confess," he writes, "I was half scandalised, and it seemed to me that thou wert dealing tyrannically with me; for I was taking measure only of my own strength, and did not perceive that thou wert first treating the whole matter silently with God. Not only was no companion given to help me, but, as it happened to the children of Israel in Egypt, the labor was increased and no straw supplied."

He concludes, however, with a grand gesture of thanksgiving. Alluding to the fact that Philip's tomb was already shining with tablets and silver votive offerings, "bright testimonies of thy miracles," he offers Philip the most splendid offering of all. He hopes that his dedication will be allowed to hang there with the rest. And so to this day it does.

What we must remember is how Philip came to set Baronius to his task. From 1552 to 1574 there appeared the thirteen volumes popularly known as the *Centuries of Magdeburg* in which the Lutheran reformers tried to press history into the service of their revolt. At first their work created a sensation, for there was no ecclesiastical history written by a Catholic on a comparable scale, so that it seemed that history was the greatest of the weapons of Protestantism. St. Robert Bellarmine did something to meet the attack, and in 1567 St. Peter Canisius was commissioned by the Pope to undertake a refutation.[1] In 1571 a group of

---

[1] In 1568 Canisius was in Rome to make some researches and at this time he used to go to the Oratory to listen to Baronius.

Catholic scholars was also appointed to make a still more complete refutation. But as Pius V, who had appointed them, died the following year, little was accomplished except a refutation on particular points. Philip perceived, however, that something more than this piecemeal effort was needed. The only thing that would do was a Catholic history that should be comprehensive and whose scholarship could not be questioned.

In 1557 there had appeared a manual of Church history written by an Augustinian friar named Onofrio Panvinio. And no doubt it was upon this book that Baronius had first to base himself when, as a callow layman of twenty-two, he began his addresses at the Oratory. But Philip would not allow him to depend on it too much or too long. Nor, for that matter, was Baronius the kind of man who would have been content with that. Lady Amabel Kerr well describes his methods when she says, "He sought verifications of his facts in every direction, and even dead stones came to life under his touch and had their tale to tell. There was scarcely a building or a ruin in Rome, scarcely a monument, pagan or Christian, which did not speak to him. Every inscription was studied and dissected; and the relics in the churches, their history, antecedents and authenticity were gone into and made use of for his work. Thus during those long years of preparation, his insight grew more keen and his perception more unerring, till the day came when the harvest was ripe, and ready to be stored in the written volumes."

Philip not only gave Baronius very slight help in the writing of the *Annals* — except that of insisting that they be written — he even seemed at times to go out of his way to make things difficult for the historian. So often was Baronius assigned to kitchen duty — far more often than his turn came — that he wrote over the fireplace with a piece

of charcoal, *Baronius, coquus perpetuus.* It was in the kitchen
that learned visitors who called to see him — perhaps St.
Peter Canisius was one of these — would find him in an
apron and with his shirt-sleeves rolled up scouring pots and
pans. When in later years the boys and young men made a
noise in the community house — they often played tennis
against the wall of Philip's room — and Baronius and others
of the Fathers made a most reasonable protest that they
were being disturbed by the infernal din, Philip would
simply tell the youths, "Pay no attention to what they say.
Go on with your play." And to a visitor who expressed
his wonder that Philip would endure the uproar, the famous
answer was made, "They may chop wood on my back, so
long as they commit no sin." Unquestionably a beautiful
remark, but one that hardly furthered the studies of poor
Baronius. And when in spite of all the difficulties, Baronius
published a new volume and took it to Philip — looking for
a few words of praise — all that he ever got was an obedience to serve thirty Masses.

Baronius took it all with touching humility. He came to
realize what was Philip's purpose, though at the time he
was often hurt and puzzled by the treatment given him.
Philip even seemed to take a mischievous delight in making
him ridiculous. Once at a wedding at which they were both
present, Philip told him to intone the *Miserere.* Another
time he sent him out with a very large bottle to buy wine.
He had orders first to sample the entire stock of the merchants, and after asking them to wash the bottle out and
purchasing a minuscule amount of wine, he was to give a
gold coin and demand change. Yet then, as always, Baronius
did just what Philip told him to do. When he came down
with fever, Philip sent him word that he was to order it to
leave him. Even then Baronius obeyed. Full of simplicity,

he said, "Fever, I command you on behalf of the Father to go away." Then at once he got up and dressed, perfectly cured.

Philip, however, now and then appeared to be on the verge of carrying things a bit too far. When in 1592 Clement VIII gave the historian a pension of four hundred scudi a year to pay for the publication of the *Annals,* Philip insisted that Baronius should now comply with the Oratorian rule and contribute to the expenses of the house. This put Baronius in a quandary. He did not see how he could in conscience use any part of the Pope's money for a purpose other than the one for which it was intended. Philip, however, was adamant. He made it plain that Baronius must obey or leave the Congregation, so that Baronius thought he had no other choice but to go. But before reaching a final decision, he consulted his friend Tomaso Bozio, who advised him to do what Philip said. The moment Baronius told Philip that he would do so, Philip laughed and answered, "Oh, I don't want any of your money! All I wanted was your obedience." He had amused himself at the expense of Baronius and had at the same time given him a lesson in humility. With that he was perfectly satisfied. He always knew when he had gone far enough; at that point his tact made him stop. Of course, he had never had the slightest intention of letting Baronius leave.

Philip at other times behaved in such a way that anyone less devoted than Baronius would have fled from the Congregation. It was bad enough that he would never make any comment on the merits of the *Annals,* what was intolerable was that he let it be known that he had assigned young Antonio Gallonio to examine what Baronius had written and to correct its mistakes. When Gallonio, gaily sailing in, did discover what he believed were a few errors,

Baronius was deeply troubled. It was characteristic of his noble spirit that, as he wrote to his confidant, Antonio Talpa, at Naples, he would rather die than defend himself against a brother-Oratorian. "That I have written the *Annals* at all," he says in conclusion, "is, as I know, solely and entirely the gift of God. To Him therefore be all glory, and to me humiliation."

The glory of Baronius, nevertheless, spread through the world; it was inevitable that honors should come to him. Though he several times managed to evade the bishopric with which he was threatened, after Philip's death Clement VIII insisted on making him a cardinal. It was in vain that Baronius protested; the Pope grew (or pretended to grow) angry and peremptorily ordered him to accept the dignity under pain of excommunication. Only then did he submit. It was in tears that he was led from the room by young Cardinal Aldobrandini, who had been educated as a boy at the Oratory, to be vested in his robes.

Even after that he went back to the Oratory as often as he could. When he did so, he laid aside all marks of the cardinalate and took his turn at waiting at table. Sometimes, too, in the papal palace, he used to snatch his red hat from his head and throw it to the person nearest to him, crying, "Take it to the Pope and never let me see it again!" Yet a cardinal he had to remain, though within his apartments he had a little wooden cell constructed in which he lived in absolute poverty. When attendants were forced upon him, he used to kneel every night before the one who was supposed to be his personal body-servant and take off his shoes. Philip had humbled him; now he did everything he could to humiliate himself.

Twice he was nearly elected Pope, once at the conclave of 1605 which ended by choosing Leo XI, and again after

Leo's death in the same year. Then the cardinals tried to drag him into the Pauline Chapel and make him Pope by acclamation. He had to cling to a pillar and cry, "I will not be pope! I will not be pope!" Soon afterwards he was permitted to lay down his burden and, a simple Oratorian Father once more, to return to his brethren. Among them he died. He and the brilliant Tarugi — who became a cardinal like himself, and also resigned all his dignities before the end — lie in the Vallicella side by side in death.

The whole of the lives of these two remarkable men was moulded by Philip. Tarugi used to say in his old age that for fifty years he had been Philip's novice. But the truth is that, devoted as he was to the founder of the Oratory, he often opposed him and was of the party that would have turned the Oratory into something that Philip had never had in mind — a religious order. He did not succeed, but at any rate he showed that he lacked something of the Philippine spirit. In Baronius that spirit was always perfectly exemplified; he was the complete Oratorian. It was only because he was so complete an Oratorian, so docile a disciple, that Philip was able to make him into an historian.

Chapter Eight

THE CHURCH OF THE FLORENTINES

A T THE beginning of September, 1563, Philip became
so ill that he was thought to be dying. Even his rallies
were regarded by his doctors as the last flicker of the flame.
He did in fact sink after them, so that he was anointed four
times in expectation of death. It was only Philip who was
quite sure that he was going to recover. He kept saying that
he was not yet prepared to appear before God and that,
as he had received so many other graces from Him, he was
going to get the grace of getting well. He always maintained that spiritual persons were given an intimation of
their end; he had received none. His prediction of recovery
proved sound; he was up by the close of the year and at
work again.

It had been almost like this with him at the close of the
previous year. Then he had collapsed — from the burden of
his labors, people, naturally enough, supposed. But Philip
knew better; it was rather that the perpetual exaltation in
which he lived became every now and then too much. The
fervor by which he was assailed quite literally shook him
to pieces. All through his life he laughed at his doctors, even
while obeying them; and he often told them that his "dis-
ease" was something they could neither diagnose nor cure.
He still had more than twenty years of life before him. Had

he died then, he would have been regarded as a saint by his many disciples, but he would probably never have been canonized, if for no other reason than that he was still somewhat under a cloud of official suspicion. The exercises of the Oratory were as yet far from having received general approval.

His death at that time would, for that matter, have made his work a mere flash in the pan. The Congregation of the Oratory to be founded by him — the organization destined to perpetuate his work — had not as yet been thought of. Much had to be done by him before he left the world, and though in his humility he did not permit himself to believe that he was needed, he was at least certain that he was going to live.

He had been in difficulties during the reign of Paul IV, and he was to be in difficulties again during that of Pius V. Now the milder interregnum of Pius IV (1559–1565) gave him the chance to consolidate what he had begun. And in the cardinal-nephew, St. Charles Borromeo, he had found a most powerful backer, one who was to be invaluable to him in the dark days ahead. He knew that he would not die yet.

When Gianangelo de' Medici was elected pope, his nephew, Charles Borromeo, who was only twenty-two and not yet a priest, was at once summoned to Rome, created a Cardinal, and appointed Archbishop of Milan, Secretary of State and Papal Legate of the Romagna. Between this young man and Philip — though they were very unlike in everything except sanctity — a great intimacy grew up, and in spite of misunderstandings that might easily have wrecked any friendship, it lasted until the untimely death of Charles in 1584. Had it not been for Charles, the work at the Oratory might have been suppressed.

The favoritism of a papal uncle for his nephew had time after time proved a bad thing for the Church. That it could come very close to being disastrous had been shown in a specially striking way under the previous pontificate, when the nephews of the rigid Paul IV (of all people!) had given such grave scandal. The scandals had, in fact, been so enormous that nepotism, in its older form, was made an impossibility ever afterwards. Cardinal-nephews continued to be the fashion, and were, after all, an administrative convenience; but the indiscriminate advancing of members of the pope's family to positions of secular authority — that much at least disappeared. Even in promoting Borromeo, Pius IV must have caused some misgivings. But this time nepotism turned out to be providential. Here was a cardinal-nephew who completely fulfilled the ideal. If he gave any scandal, it was, as the Abbé Ponnelle puts it, "a kind of scandal [occasioned by] his austerity, his purity, and his application to work." Even his recreations in the *Noctes Vaticanae* were edifying. They consisted in the holding at the end of the day of an academy by which St. Charles hoped to increase the range of his knowledge and his facility in public speaking. The Venetian Ambassador was to write of him in 1565: "He . . . leads so edifying a life in every way that he forms a remarkable example. One may say with perfect truth that he has more effect upon the court of Rome than all the decrees of the Council." Well was Charles Borromeo styled in the bull of his canonization issued by Paul V, "the model of Catholic bishops!"

He was, indeed, the very embodiment of the spirit of the Council of Trent. Ludwig von Pastor says, "if anyone wished to draw a picture of a reformer of the Church, it would surely take the form of Borromeo." At his funeral oration the Franciscan Panigarola had not greatly exaggerated when he declared that the saint "had enjoyed no more of his wealth than a dog enjoys the riches of his master, namely a little water, bread and straw." His vast archiepiscopal palace at Milan was conducted like a religious community, with the aristocratic Archbishop as the most ascetic of its members. Few men can ever have accomplished more than St. Charles did in the brief forty-eight years of his life.

But what matters here is his friendship with Philip Neri. That the friendship should have been formed at all is a little curious, for though Bacci says, very truly as concerns Philip, that he had an amiable disposition, a winning appearance, and a wonderful power of attracting men, yet he is not nearly so correct when he proceeds to the generalisation that such are "qualities which are usually found in those who are chosen to gain souls to God." Humanly attractive qualities are not invariably found in the saints; and Charles Borromeo — with the thin, tense face and the overprominent hooked nose that appear in his portraits — did not have much of Philip's personal charm. If they were drawn to each other, it was for supernatural reasons. On the natural plane Charles met with much that puzzled him in his friend. Always the great lord himself, he was frequently startled by Philip's freedom of speech and behavior, and even tried to get Philip to comport himself in what he considered a more dignified manner. In spite of this they had to the end a profound veneration for each other. That Charles had this veneration for Philip was to be the salvation of the Oratory.

Philip, however, never cultivated Charles because he happened to be influential. If he was drawn to him, it was because he recognised a saint. But for that matter, Philip never relied on the good offices of the highly placed or sought any favors for himself. A story which belongs to a later period (1590) may be told here to illustrate his attitude. Cardinal Bonelli (generally known as Cardinal Alessandrino, as had been his uncle, Pius V before him), had many times offered to promote Philip's interests, always to have his offers declined. Meeting the Cardinal one day, Philip reminded him of this and went on, "But now I would like to ask a favor of your Most Illustrious Lordship, only I know you will not grant it." "Why not?" "Oh no, you won't," Philip insisted. This went on for several minutes until at last the Cardinal said, "Tell me what it is. I will do it for you." Then came Philip's joke: "Well, I would like your Most Illustrious Lordship to give me the secret of making my beard black." His was a beard that by then had been snow-white for many years.

Nor did Philip cultivate the Dominicans at the Minerva for any other reason than that he had admired the order from the time he knew the friars at San Marco's in Florence. Yet they were not only in a position to do him some services with the Dominican Pope Pius V, but they were also under an obligation to him for what he had done for them when the condemnation of the writings of Savonarola had appeared certain. The community he founded and their own became almost one. The style of preaching at the Oratory was imitated at the Minerva, and Philip was often invited to be present at the clothing of their novices — many of whom he had sent to them — and was given a share in all the spiritual works of the Friars Preachers. It does not appear that he was ever formally a Dominican tertiary, but he was virtually one. He even became almost a kind of second novice-master to the young friars, and often took them out on little picnics. On these occasions the abstemious old man would encourage the novices to eat and grow fat. "It makes me fat," he assured them, "to see you eat!" Delighted with his humorous conversation and his stories, with which, as was his way, he somehow contrived to mingle piety, he would take them back at the end of the day to their cloister. He was given the key to the place, so that he could let himself in at any time, and there he used to go now and then with his musicians into the choir-stalls and sing Compline with the friars, a Compline which on those evenings ended with a *Salve*, not in plain-chant but in a part-song setting by Animuccia.

Though this friendship may have stood him in good stead with Pius V, he never once tried to exploit it. Never could there be any question in anybody's mind about that. He might be accused of introducing dangerous novelties at the Oratory, but the only man who ever suggested that he was not perfectly disinterested was Paul IV's Vicar, Cardinal Rosario. However much the staid may have frowned on Philip's eccentricities, the eccentricities themselves showed how indifferent he was about currying favor. On the contrary, they were often deliberately designed to lessen people's good opinion of him.

It is, however, clear from the outset that while Philip had his detractors, he also had fervent admirers. He had had them even before he became a priest, in the years when he worked as a free-lance among the young men in the banks and the business houses. After his priesthood, when the possibilities of his work were so vastly extended, the admirers grew still more numerous and devoted. A notable sign of this was his being asked by the large Florentine community in Rome to take charge of the important Florentine church there.

In 1519 they had obtained an establishment of ten priests to minister to their spiritual needs at San Giovanni dei Fiorentini, a handsome church designed by no less a person than Michelangelo. When in 1562 the superior of this group died, the Florentines turned to Philip, as a brother-Florentine, and tried to induce him to accept the supervision of their church. Though he once told one of the Sisters at the Tor di Specchi, "My country is heaven," he did not wish to imply that he was completely indifferent to ordinary attachments. The Florentines at all events were sure that he was the man they wanted.

At first he refused their offer. He did not wish to accept a pastoral charge, as he thought it would mean that he would have to give up the Oratory. In any case he did not want to leave San Girolamo. Not until 1564 was a compromise effected. That the Florentines persisted and that they were willing to meet Philip's terms shows how eager they were to get him. Philip might go on living at San Girolamo, where he could conduct the Oratory as before; but he agreed to supply San Giovanni with chaplains from among his own disciples. These were not to separate themselves from the Oratory; on the contrary they were expected to attend its exercises every day. They might, however, serve the Florentine church; and he would accept the office of rector. Even that much was effected only because the Florentines induced the Pope to tell Philip that this was his desire. The compromise effected left the Oratory as Philip's main work.

The priests he sent the Florentines — the newly ordained Bordini and Baronius and Alessandro Fedeli, who were joined soon afterwards by Tarugi and the gentle Angelo Velli — were not to be detached from him, and he was to remain where he was. The arrangement was a curious one and depended wholly upon the voluntary consent of those who accepted it. As Capecelatro says, "While they lived at San Giovanni their hearts were still at San Girolamo, and they drew from Philip the inspiration of all their plans and desires, as well as their souls' life. Every morning they went to San Girolamo to confess to Philip; in the afternoon they went again to hear the customary sermons, or to preach in their turn; and again in the evening they went a third time for meditation and the exercises in the Oratory." There were obvious difficulties and inconveniences in such a mode of life. Nevertheless, this was the only plan that Philip would entertain. He was absolutely determined not to appear publicly as the rector of San Giovanni by residing there with them.

Yet in spite of Philip, the formation of a new congregation was now being forced upon him by circumstances. The very fact of there being a community life at San Giovanni obliged him to make some simple regulations, few as these were, even though they were not to be considered as having the force of a religious rule. Ponnelle truly remarks: "The life of the community at St. John's was really the springtime of the Congregation of the Oratory, of which no one had as yet thought."

The only way all this affected the Oratory itself was that on Saturdays the exercises were no longer held, for then the Fathers at San Giovanni beat the carpets and washed the floor of the church; while doing so, they could not also be at the meetings of San Girolamo. But every day they had to cook and serve their own food, taking turns at the task, though on this account they were not excused from attendance at the Oratory. It was during this period that Baronius obtained his celebrity as cook in perpetuity for the group of five — seven if we count the boys Germanico Fedeli and Ottavio Paravicini, whom Baronius was tutoring and who read aloud to the priests in the refectory.

As Philip's priests were now serving a Florentine church,

some concessions had to be made to Florentine customs. Instead of preaching seated, they had to use the pulpit, and· to wear there the wide cotta beloved by Florentines but hitherto never used by them. Moreover, a certain amount of formality and even elaborateness had to be put into their oratorical style, as that was what the Florentines demanded. At San Girolamo they still adhered to the original simplicity and conversational tone.

Though Philip now appeared to have divided himself, the Oratory continued to be his main work, and the pastoral charge assumed by him at San Giovanni turned out to be his main means for perpetuating what he had begun. It turned out so because it resulted in the founding of a religious congregation. Had it not been for San Giovanni, Philip would probably never have established such a thing at all. The seeming division of activity therefore brought about a greater coherence in the end.

Philip, however, was by no means out of all his difficulties. At the end of 1565 Pius IV died and was succeeded by Pius V. The new Pope, the last of all the popes to have been canonized, was so suspicious of what was going on at the Oratory that, as we know from a letter written by Charles Borromeo to his agent, Nicolò Ormaneto, on January 29, 1567, he was seriously thinking of suppressing the Oratory. It is rather strange that the work of one saint came close to being wrecked by another saint; but such was the fact. To understand how this happened we must try to understand the mood of the times and the character of Pius V.

Transparently sincere himself, he was in a world full of people who were rather disingenuous in their loud talk about reform. They wished to ingratiate themselves with the new regime by exhibiting themselves as zealous reformers. Now that apostolic simplicity was the order of the day, the cunning devised subtle means for satisfying a greed they had formerly had to satisfy by cruder methods. The old avenues of advancement having been closed, they had to open new avenues for themselves. One of the best was that of delating other people to the authorities.

Nor was this all. The very fact that there were ecclesiastical circles in which it almost seemed that a premium was set upon hypocrisy gave hypocrites an opportunity to denounce hypocrisy. Ponnelle describes the situation: "Men to whom ambition was the mainspring of their lives and the end of their existence found themselves driven to a life of disinterestedness; and more than that: it was on this foundation of disinterestedness that they had to build up the edifice of their hopes. In fact, the higher they hoped to climb the more modest and humble they must appear to be." In order to cover their own craft they were clever enough to suggest that Philip's disciples were trying to further their ambitions by the device of a nauseous parade of piety.

Even this was not all. Many people whose sincerity cannot be questioned still had serious doubts as to the advisability of permitting laymen to preach at the Oratory. Such a practice might be very picturesque and attractive, but was open to obvious dangers. There was not much use in arguing that these laymen were not really "preaching" at all but were merely talking in an informal way, not in a church but in a separate building. The fact remained that untrained men, however gifted and well-intentioned they might be, were always liable to fall into theological inaccuracies. The reply that Philip kept them from talking about speculative matters and insisted on their seeking to foment fervor or dealing with practical considerations or the lives of the saints was not accepted as quite satisfactory. For it was of course impossible always to avoid theology, and it was known that Philip sometimes had to get up after a speaker had finished and, in his gentle way, correct his mistakes. Why allow people to preach who could fall into such errors? Inexactitude was all the more inevitable because of the speakers' being encouraged to make, instead of formal and carefully prepared addresses, those that were spontaneous and improvised according to their "inspiration." It was felt that the "freshness" that the Oratory sought was being obtained at too high a price.

Baronius was, it is true, a priest now, but until recently he had been preaching as a layman. Tarugi was not yet a priest. And though the two doctors, Modio and Fucci, who had discoursed so eloquently on the lives of the saints were now dead, others had taken their places, among them the convert rabbi, Andrea del Monte, who was expatiating learnedly on the "Old Law." That fact alone would have made Pius V, who was severe against Jews, somewhat uneasy. He had just driven them out of the papal states and tolerated them in Rome only on condition that they kept to their ghetto and wore a distinguishing yellow cap. Philip, on the other hand, showed a special tenderness toward members of this race, many of whom he converted. His interest in them was hardly calculated to ingratiate him with the Pope.

Others factors operated. Pius was mortally afraid that Italy might be convulsed by a war of religion, such as had torn France apart. And he knew that in Italy Protestantism was all the more dangerous because it did not openly declare itself, and that the doctrines of the reformers were sometimes being preached in Catholic pulpits. It was for this reason that he had set the Inquisition to work to ferret out all such insidious heretical tendencies. Later he was to grow more moderate in this matter, as is shown by the fact that from 1569 to 1572 there were only two autos da fé in Rome; but during the early part of his reign he was very much concerned with the suppression of heresy. He could hardly ignore reports that the "Lutheran pest" had infected the Oratory.

Many things that Philip said and did must be admitted to have been all too likely to excite the Pope's suspicions. Pius V had gone so far in his loyal admiration for Paul IV — he had nearly taken the name Paul himself by way of showing that he was the continuator of his policies — as to bring about a judicial rehabilitation of the executed Carafa and even to see to it that the procurator-fiscal, Pallantieri, who had so savagely accused them, should himself be executed for calumny and heresy.[1] That Philip was a friend of Pallantieri and assisted him in his last moments, with an expression of belief in his innocence, did not increase his standing with the Pope. Nor, if it comes to that, was Philip's subsequent protest in favor of the gypsies and vagabonds whom Pius had rounded up for the galleys, the act of a man who wished to curry official favor. Though on this occasion the Pope yielded, he probably did not feel any better disposed toward those who had forced him to change his mind.

Yet Philip recognised that Pius was a saint, even while disapproving of certain aspects of his policy. It was true

---

[1] The implication of the Duke of Paliano in the murder of his wife was confessed by him, though she was actually strangled by her brother. That Cardinal Carlo Carafa may have been an accessory is probable. The quashing of the verdict, however, did not touch the murder but dealt only with other matters. While the Carafa were a thoroughly bad set, their prosecution had been in many ways unjust and vindictive, for they had been made to pay for the misdeeds of many of the papal favorites of the past. Moreover, Philip II took this opportunity for settling old political scores. The whole case is complicated, but the verdict was of too sweeping a character to be allowed to stand as it was.

that the Pope was not a skilled secular statesman in the
sense of Pius IV; with him nothing mattered except the
kingdom of God, and here he committed what history — and
Pius V himself in later life — came to see to be tactical
errors, as in the ineffectual bull of excommunication launched
against Elizabeth of England in 1570.[2] The methods of the
two men were very dissimilar.

Pius, however, though he took Paul IV as his model, was
without Paul's violence and irascibility. His reign was severe
but was not a reign of terror. Not only was his personal life
one of extreme holiness but he had a great deal of kindli-
ness and amiability. One small instance of this appeared in
the case of that humble disciple of Philip's known as "il
Ferrarese" who lived by making and selling small plaster
images of the saints. The Pope having forbidden such a
traffic, because no doubt abuses had crept in, the poor man
knelt before Pius one day with his wares on the steps of
St. Peter's and begged permission to go on with what was
his only means of livelihood. The Pope glanced down at the
tray at his feet and exclaimed, "What, would you sell Christ!"
With a happy inspiration of tact "il Ferrarese" took up the
image and said, "Take it, Your Holiness; I give it to you."
He was given permission to continue his trade.

To return to the Oratory: though Philip had escaped condemnation in 1559 at the end of the reign of Paul IV, he
was still somewhat under a cloud. Thus one day in 1563
Cardinal Morone, whom Paul IV had imprisoned on a suspicion of heresy but who had just been appointed Legate
to the Council of Trent, stopped Philip while he was walk-

---

[2] It could be argued, however, that this blunder proved providential. The
Bull of Excommunication left Elizabeth unharmed and did make the position
of her Catholic subjects very difficult, but it initiated the heroic age of
English Catholicism.

ing in the street with a number of his disciples and accused him of pride and ambition for going about attended in this way. When Philip had his faculties suspended in 1559 he had cried, "I am a son of obedience!" It seemed again, all through 1567 to 1570, that now in obedience he might have to abandon his work at the Oratory. The novel devotions there, the preaching of laymen, and the free spirit animating those who attended — all this was quite enough to cause the authorities to look at them askance. As Capecelatro says, "These charges were at first whispered about with expressions of regret, but care was taken that they should reach the ear of the Pope." There were many people who were genuinely disturbed; there were still more who found this an easy way of putting their zeal for reform on display.

Fortunately Philip found in Cardinal Charles Borromeo a powerful protector. It was largely due to Borromeo that Pius owed his election, and though now the Cardinal did not have the same degree of authority that he had possessed during the reign of his uncle, he nevertheless had considerable influence. He was able to assure the Pope as to the piety of those who frequented the Oratory, and in particular that they were not Lutherans in disguise. And when he was not in Rome but at his see of Milan he instructed his agents to see to it that His Holiness was properly informed as to the facts.

In spite of this, Pius was not completely satisfied. In 1570, therefore, he commissioned two Dominicans, Paolino Bernardini and Alessandro Franceschi, to go to the Oratory to listen to the sermons and to report to him. That he chose Dominicans for this task shows that he wished to be perfectly fair; for he was carefully avoiding men who might be enemies of Philip. On the other hand, the Dominican Pope could be sure that the two Dominicans would be conscientious in the performance of their duty and not permit friendship to excuse anything that was heretical or even dangerous. As a further precaution, he instructed each man separately. Neither had any idea that his fellow had a similar commission.

But though the reports they brought back exculpated the Oratory, reports by no means so favorable continued to be circulated, and Philip remained rather uneasy in mind. He was not yet the privileged character he was to become, one whose most fantastic behavior — inconceivable in anybody else — was regarded as a quaint but authentic mark of his sanctity. The secure establishment of the Oratory was not far off; its formal recognition came in 1575 during the pontificate of Gregory XIII. Under Pius V, while it had been saved for the moment by the efforts of St. Charles Borromeo and the Dominicans, its future remained problematical.

St. Charles therefore suggested to Philip that he transfer his activities to Milan, where he could be sure of being unmolested. It was an offer that Philip now and then, when the sky was dark overhead, was inclined to accept. True, he did not ever allow himself to despair of the outcome — no temperament could have been sunnier than his, no heart more confident in God — but even a much less sensitive man than himself would have suffered terribly. There was one hot summer day when his companion, Giovanni Antonio Lucci, records that Philip took him out for a walk and strode at such a pace in his agitation as to make keeping up with him almost impossible. When they got to St. Peter's to pray before the Volto Santo, the heavy bench at which they knelt was shaken with Philip's convulsive trembling. And on the way back by the Transpontina Vecchia, Philip told Lucci all that he was suffering.

His pain was not caused only by the accusations brought

against him. It was due also to the prospect of his having to leave Rome. Yet — paradoxically — he also suffered by knowing deep in his heart that he would never leave Rome or even be able to bring himself to repay St. Charles's kindness — though only to the extent of letting him have the small number of men for whom he was asking.

For he soon discovered that what Charles had in mind was a group of priests who would not be under Philip's direction but his own. The Cardinal's intention was not merely that of getting them to set up an Oratory in Milan but of using them in the work of diocesan supervision. As this would have destroyed their distinctive character, Philip — while holding on to Milan as a possible avenue of escape, should Rome become too hot for him — thought of Milan only as a last desperate resource. He continued to hope for some turn of fortune and kept putting St. Charles off — a state of affairs that dragged on for over ten years. Then St. Charles, seeing that he was never going to get any men from Philip — except Tassone, who had been sent in 1567 and soon withdrawn, and a group supplied later and also quickly taken back — determined to establish his own Oratory of St. Ambrose, which still exists under the name of the Oblates of St. Charles.

Cardinal Borromeo perhaps had some right to complain of broken promises, but Philip perceived that his friend did not fully understand the nature of the work he was doing, or else not the limits he had imposed upon himself. He had to be completely independent, and he had to be in Rome, at the centre of everything. Elsewhere — even in his native Florence — Philip could not have been completely Philip. Yet though the relations between the two men were subjected to some strain, their friendship never faltered. Charles came to perceive that Philip was not going to do what he wished done. As for the Philippine sense of humor, the Cardinal winced at some of its manifestations, but he never failed to see that under it lay a solid and beautiful piety. And Philip for his part always recognised the great work his friend had done and was doing for the reform of the Church.

A mark of Borromeo's confidence in Philip was shown in placing his own sister Anna in Philip's hands for spiritual direction when he left for Milan. Anna was the image of her brother, ungainly, tense, and with a much too prominent nose. Married to Fabrizio Colonna, the son of the leader of the papal forces at the battle of Lepanto, she had the world at her feet. Yet she was tormented by fantastic scruples and could not bring herself to consummate her marriage, much as she wanted children. When at last she did bear two sons, after Philip had resolved her doubts and prophesied her motherhood, she considered his predictions marvellous and used to say that, in some sense, her children were Philip's because of his prayers. Even her mother-in-law talked in the same strain, and when Philip visited the Colonna palace and the boys ran to greet him, their grandmother would cry, "They are yours, Father Philip; they are yours!"

Philip often had to treat Anna a little severely. Once, after she had gone to confession to him, she came back again within an hour, and Philip, with that roughness he now and then assumed, ordered her away. On another occasion when she knelt and asked him for his blessing, Philip deliberately placed his hand on her head in such a way as to loosen all her elaborately dressed hair. He was pleased that she took this mortification meekly. All the same, the good woman must often have been a trial to him, even if he also inflicted humiliations on her. No doubt her brother the Cardinal-Archbishop was aware that Anna needed the kind of handling that was so characteristic of Philip. In any event what was imposed on Philip's women penitents was mild compared to what was imposed on his young men.

There are many other indications of the perfect confidence Philip and Charles had in one another, despite their failing sometimes to fall in with each other's plans. Though Philip was unable to supply Charles with any men during the reign of Pius V — much less to transfer the whole Oratory to Milan — he was at least able to recommend many ecclesiastics to the Cardinal, who was always glad to employ them and always found them satisfactory. It was worthy of note that this supposedly eccentric character was never at fault in his judgment of men. His unerring instinct in this matter was therefore implicitly trusted, not only by St. Charles but by all the people who knew him well.

St. Charles, for his part, was eager that the agents he kept at Rome should maintain close contact with Philip and that they should lodge at San Girolamo or near by. It was his express wish that the Milanese whom he sent to the city should frequent the Oratory and, if possible, take Philip as their confessor. His attitude appears in the letter he wrote to Alessandro Simonetta, one of them: "After you have experienced even a little of [the society of the Fathers at San Girolamo] I am sure that there will be no need to use compulsion to make you return there." The Cardinal always expected these broad hints of his to be acted upon promptly.

While it is probable that during the last years of the pontificate of Pius V there were a certain number of habitués of the Oratory who dropped away, for fear that their attendance might damage their prospects, the numbers of those who went do not seem to have been greatly affected. Their devotion to Philip was so firm that they even seem to have been drawn all the closer to him because he was under a cloud. If the pilgrimages and picnics had become less popular — in contrast to the vast crowds we hear of going to them when Pius IV was on the papal throne — this was in all likelihood because they had been largely made up of men who did not regularly frequent the other exercises and were only on the fringe of Philip's movement. Moreover, these things were now less of a novelty, and Philip had less need of stressing this particular method for providing an attraction to the Carnival. The rigid Pope himself saw to it that the Carnival was decorously conducted.

To obtain men who would frequent the exercises there was no longer any need for Philip to do what he had done in past years and hunt them up in the university or business section; they came now of their own accord, and among them were many fine gentlemen and prelates, though Philip remained careful not to let the Oratory become a meeting-place only for a social and intellectual elite. Anybody could go, and all were on an equal footing. If the biographers, by mentioning people of distinction so frequently, convey the impression that they constituted the whole body of those attending, this is certainly not Philip's fault. It was only natural that well-known names should be recorded and that the many obscure persons present should be passed over in silence; the eminent respectability of the Oratory gatherings had to be shown in this way. Unfortunately some of the best born among them had most to live down, as in the case of Fabrizio de' Massimi, one of the earliest and closest of Philip's desciples. His brother Flaminio had stabbed their sister Plautilia to death.

Philip and the Oratory survived the pontificate of Pius V, though it is quite possible that they might not have done so had that Pope reigned much longer. A saint and a great reformer — one providential to the Church even if his politi-

cal judgment was sometimes bad — he could operate effec-
tually, under the circumstances, only by employing rigor;
and this was something that was a perpetual danger to the
unconventional Philip. It is probable that all suspicion would
have been removed had Philip and Pius known one another
intimately. But there was nothing of that warm friendship
that came to exist between Philip and the later popes.
Capecelatro tells, indeed, a pleasant story of Philip and Pius
making a rosary together, but the Abbé Ponnelle points out
that there is no definite proof that there was even so much
as an acquaintance. If the Oratory was saved this was mainly
because of the powerful influence of St. Charles Borromeo
and, to a lesser extent, that of the Dominicans at the
Minerva.

In 1572 Pius died and the conclave elected Cardinal Ugo
Boncompagni as his successor. Philip predicted his election,
but perhaps this was not so very marvellous. He must have
known that the general mood was for a Pope less stern than
the one who had just died, and that the chances of Boncompagni were excellent. Much more striking had been his
foretelling not only that Cardinal Alessandrino (Michele
Ghislieri) would be elected in 1566 but the day and the
time of the day when the conclave would reach its decision.
In the case of Gregory XIII it hardly needed a supernatural
revelation to guess who would be the choice of the cardinals.
The very name Ugo Boncompagni suggested a milder rule,
for was he not *buon compagno,* a good companion, a good
fellow?

Gregory was unquestionably a milder ruler than his predecessor, but anybody who looked for a total reversal of
policy was disappointed. The old man with the sad face
and the long white beard often seen by Montaigne in the
streets of Rome in 1580 riding his white richly caparisoned

horse, which even then, when he was nearing eighty, he could mount without any help from a groom, was destined to have a long reign and one that was specially fortunate for Philip, who became his intimate friend. It was under Gregory that the Oratory was to be founded.

Yet just before this happened, it looked for a moment as though Philip and the priests associated with him were about to be absorbed by one of the religious orders. This was when a group of one of the newly-founded Clerks Regular, the Barnabites, came to Rome in 1574 and lived, pending the time when they could obtain permanent quarters, at San Girolamo. By then the priests who were under Philip's direction had by degrees advanced so far toward the definite organization that was to come the following year that some of Philip's associates were strongly in favor of incorporating themselves with the young order. The transition looked easy and natural, so that the Barnabite Tito degli Alessi could write to his General on November 13 of Philip: "He seems to be almost as much one of us as if we were of [their] Fathers. . . . They treat us quite as if we were of their own community." He wrote again the following February 12 to say: "The Fathers are so affectionate and cordial towards us, that it seems as if they wished to form one body with us." All of which was no doubt true of some of the Fathers, though Philip's cordiality implied nothing of the kind. He had always been perfectly clear in his own mind that he did not wish to join any order. Alessi goes on to say that the matter had been mentioned several times, and that on one occasion Monsignor Speciano, the agent of St. Charles, had said that if Philip joined the Barnabites, he would do so too. Philip, however, returned the evasive answer: "It is a good thing to change from an evil life to a good one; but to change from a good state to a better is something that should be considered thoroughly and for a long time." His courtesy forbade him to give an outright refusal; his modesty made him concede that the mode of life of the Barnabites was higher than his own.

The fact is of course that, however akin he might be to the Barnabites in spirit, his aims and theirs were altogether different. That was something that some of his disciples did not always fully grasp. Then and in the years to come they often pressed upon Philip the idea of a congregation that could be used as a reforming agency in the Church. This was not his idea at all. The only reformation he considered himself as called upon to effect was one in the lives of individuals. And the only association he envisaged was one of men held together by nothing save the bond of charity; religious vows were absolutely ruled out: without vows they were to aim at the perfection of the monastic life. The good Alessi never ceased to hope; he should have known from the outset that Philip would never become a Barnabite.

But if Philip tactfully evaded all the advances of Alessi, there occurred in Easter Week of 1574 an event which — as we can see now — made the founding of the Oratory inevitable. This was the transferring of the exercises from the attic of San Girolamo — which could not seat more than a hundred men at most — to the new and commodious Oratory built at San Giovanni dei Fiorentini. For it was the giving of these exercises at San Giovanni which aroused a criticism from which he had so far been spared there; and such criticism made him see that it was necessary to secure a church where he could be completely independent. Until then San Giovanni had known Philip's priests only as chaplains; the coming of the Oratory, though this was something for which they had explicitly asked, changed the situation.

Yet when the Colonna offered Philip a church at this very

time, Philip let the Barnabites have it instead. This was a very characteristic instance of his courtesy; at the same time there may also have been some shrewdness in the renunciation. By this way he got rid of the Barnabites and the pressure they were bringing to bear upon him. It always embarrassed him to have to refuse anybody anything.

Of the exercises as conducted in the new Oratory we have an account in a letter written on May 28, 1576, by Giovanni Giovenale Ancina — who was to be beatified in 1890 — to his brother, Giovanni Matteo, who became like himself a member of Philip's Congregation. "For some time past," he writes, "I have been going to the Oratory of San Giovanni dei Fiorentini, where they deliver every day most beautiful discourses on the Gospel, or on the virtues and vices, or the lives of the saints. There are four or five who preach every day, and bishops, prelates, and other persons of distinction go to hear them. At the conclusion there is a little music to console and recreate the mind, which is fatigued by the preceding discourse. They have gone through the life of the glorious St. Francis and those of his first disciples, and of St. Antony of Padua. I assure you it is a most delightful exercise, and a most consoling and edifying thing; and I regret very much that neither you nor I knew of this noble and holy practice last year. You must know too that those who deliver the discourses are men of distinction, in holy orders, and of most exemplary and spiritual lives. Their superior is a certain Father Philip, an old man of sixty, but wonderful in many respects, and especially for holiness of life and for his astonishing prudence and skill in inventing and promoting spiritual exercises. He was the author of that great work of charity done at the Trinità dei Pellegrini during the last jubilee. . . . They say he is an oracle not only in Rome but in the most distant parts of Italy and in France and Spain, so that many come to him for counsel; in a word, he is another Ruysbroeck or Thomas à Kempis or Tauler."

The only change we notice in this from the accounts left by Baronius and others is that the addresses are no longer made by laymen. Partly this may have been due to the fact that the former lay preachers were either dead — like Modio and Fucci — or, like Baronius and Tarugi, had become priests. But another reason was that, after the criticism that had been received on account of laymen being permitted to preach, it had seemed advisable to stop that practice.

It is evident, however, that the work was still wholly based on Philip himself, and that his disciples lived in a state of personal dependence upon him. That this was so is no doubt a very high tribute to Philip's attractiveness, but it is questionable whether it was entirely good for the disciples themselves. Had Philip died before 1575 it could hardly have been otherwise than that his work would have died with him. The creation of an institute was necessary for its perpetuation. The pressure of circumstances brought this about. It was not at all of Philip's own choosing.

Chapter Nine

THE FOUNDING OF THE CON-
GREGATION

NOT because Philip wished to give up San Giovanni did he do so; it was because he saw that this could not be avoided if he was to have his work undisturbed. The change came about in this way: at San Giovanni there was a priest — presumably one of the unattached men employed there in purely parochial duties — whose conduct was not all that it should have been and so resulted in his dismissal. What he had done we do not know, nor do we know his name. All that we are told is that he went to the wardens who governed San Giovanni for the Florentines and brought some charges — we are not informed what — against Philip. We can, however, surmise that these consisted of the old accusations of novelty and dangerous unconventionality, with perhaps the insinuation of heresy. Coming as they did from a priest who had been living in the house, they could not be disregarded. The man had to be listened to, and the wardens for the most part were inclined to believe him.

Fortunately there was one man among the wardens who did not. He was Giovanni Battista Altovito, who had been mainly instrumental in persuading Philip to accept the rectorship in 1564. This solitary champion took Philip's part and managed to expose the accuser. Though a veil so discreet as to be perhaps forever impenetrable has been drawn over the affair, it is at least perfectly clear that Philip was brought by it to decide that the only course for him to follow was to obtain a center from which he could not be dislodged. Too late the Florentines repented of their threats to oust him and implored him to remain. That he could be ousted was enough to make him firm in his resolve to leave. All that he would do was to consent to stay until he had found another home. He therefore remained formally rector of San Giovanni until April, 1577, in which month he resigned. But for two years it was known that he was waiting only until another church and house were ready for him.

In Gregory XIII he had a friend who was prepared to help in any way. Indeed, it was the Pope himself who selected the place where Philip should go. Two churches were proposed. One was that of Santa Maria in Monticello, near the Strada della Regola. It was a large church and easily obtainable, but it was not very centrally situated. The other church was that of Santa Maria in Vallicella in the Contrada di Parione. Though it was in a dilapidated condition, the Pope advised Philip that it would be best for his purpose because of its good location. Actually it was best only for the Pope's purposes, because it was near the court, and he was thinking of the convenience of the courtiers. The main difficulty here was that the Vallicella was then a parish church and that the incumbent could not be ejected merely to make room for Philip. That little problem was solved by an arrangement under which the priest retired on a pension of an annual hundred and ten scudi which Philip undertook to pay. As usually happens with people on a pension or annuity, he lived an inordinately long time. But at least the retirement put Philip in possession of a church of his own.

Now at last it grew apparent, even to Philip who had hitherto always opposed the idea, that he must found a congregation to perpetuate his work. Yet it was not merely out of humility that he continued to insist that not he but God (or, as he sometimes said, Our Lady) was the true founder; for it was perfectly true that the Congregation had founded itself almost in spite of his own wishes. His part in the project was largely that of resisting all proposals that the foundation should be anything like a religious order.

In this matter the Pope acted with the utmost dispatch. In the Bull, dated July 15, 1575, that transferred Santa Maria in Vallicella to Philip, the Pope gave him what almost amounted to carte blanche with regard to the rules, which were still to be drawn up, the only stipulation being that they should be in accordance with the canons of the Council of Trent. The passage reads: "In the fulness of our apostolic authority, we grant to the Superior and the priests and clerics of the said Congregation permission and full license to make such statutes and rules for the well-being and governance of the Church and Congregation as they think fit, provided only that they be not in contravention of the canons of the Council of Trent. Let them, moreover, reform at their discretion the statutes and rules already made; let them limit them or modify them or add to them, as may appear to them expedient. And such statutes and rules, thus changed or reformed or added to, shall be approved by the Holy See, and unviolably observed by all members of the said Congregation." Gregory could hardly have gone further in an expression of confidence in Philip and his Congregation.

Though Philip probably did not think of himself as introducing something new, and still less as providing a model for other associations of the kind, his concept was, in fact, a

FOUNDING OF THE CONGREGATION

complete innovation, and one that was to mark a fresh development in what might be termed quasi-monasticism.
About this a word or two might be said at this point.

The great departure of the thirteenth century was the
modification of the monastic idea by which friars came into
being — that is, men bound by the vows of religion, but
attached to their province instead of their abbey. This was
intended to bring about a greater elasticity and mobility,
and, of course, achieved its object. Other features of the tra-
ditional monastic system were afterwards shed by the various orders of clerks-regular of the sixteenth century, the best-
known group of which is the Jesuits. These, though all their
professed were bound by solemn vows, were dispensed from
the obligation of saying office in choir, saying it instead, as
secular priests do, privately. The Fathers of the Oratory
made some attempt in 1582 to recite the office in common,
but they soon gave it up for the same reason that the clerks-
regular had given up the practice — namely, that it interfered with their other duties.[1] Philip took a further step in
getting rid of all vows, except such as are taken by every
priest. And yet he sought the spirit and cohesion of a religious order while keeping his congregation a group of secu-
lars living in community. As Dr. Pastor puts his concept:
"Charity was to be the sole bond that united the Congregation; it alone compelled its members to obey, just as though
they had been united under a vow of obedience, and to live
as though they were members of a regular order." It was a
concept destined to have a great future.

To discover the origins for Philip's idea would be inter-

---

[1] The fact that Paul IV made the Jesuits say the office in choir shows
that its abandonment still seemed a good deal of an anomaly. That the
Jesuits were before long able to rid themselves again of these duties shows
just as clearly what was the tendency of the age.

esting. He must have been influenced to a great extent by
his close contact with the Sisters of the Tor di Specchi, a
community founded by St. Frances of Rome in 1433. These
were, properly speaking, not nuns at all, for they took no
vows and had no enclosure; they were simply a number of
Benedictine Oblates who lived together, affiliated to the
monastery of Santa Maria Nuova but having the privilege
of being free from the jurisdiction of the abbot. The main
part of Philip's idea of a community is obviously derived
from that source.

Other sources, however, contributed something. He took
over from the Rule of St. Benedict his concept that each
Oratorian house should be independent and autonomous.
And he followed his beloved Dominicans in maintaining a
democratic form of government, the superior being not only
elected, but without anything distinctive attaching to his
office, and serving only for a term of three years — all of
which was very far removed from that military method
which St. Ignatius inherited from the strictly centralised
Spanish monarchy. Capecelatro also suggests that, as a good
Florentine, anything but the democratic mode would have
been repugnant to Philip. Whether or not he was actually
thinking of the commune of Florence under Savonarola,
democracy was certainly what Philip insisted upon. All the
same, the Jesuits themselves may be considered as having
contributed something to the Oratory, at least to the extent
of the provision of four Deputies to assist the Provost.

One might compare Philip's rule with that of St. Vincent
de Paul's Congregation of the Missions which, after some
difficulties, was approved in 1655. Vincent, unlike Philip,
wanted vows, but not such vows as would make his subjects
technically members of a religious order. Simple and private
vows were for him not enough; he therefore proposed, and

in the end obtained, a rule under which the vows, though privately made and not formally received by the Superior General, had nevertheless the binding force of solemn vows and were, as such, dispensable only by the Pope.

Philip's plan was far more simple and therefore was easily ratified. Any man who joined him was always free to leave, if he wished to do so. He was also to keep whatever private property he might possess, though he was expected to contribute to the expenses of the house, when this was in his power, and to live according to the spirit of poverty. Rules and regulations — these had to be, but they were reduced to a minimum and were put in the form of "this is what we do" rather than in that of "this is what you must do." Obedience was to be, like everything else, spontaneous; at the same time it was to be absolute. Those who would not obey had to leave; there was no place for them in the Congregation.

St. Charles Borromeo once asked Philip how it was that he was always obeyed so promptly and got the answer, "Because I give very few commands." It was his custom not to order his subjects to do this or do that, but instead to suggest or exhort with a "This is what I should like you to do, but if it seems too hard I will do it for you," or with a "What would you say if I imposed this charge on you?" Yet Bacci tells us that his authority was so great that he could guide people with a look and that his ordinary method of rebuke was to fix his eyes sternly on a man.

Gentle as Philip was, he could be severe to the point of ruthlessness. Nobody ever bore more heavily on his penitents than he did, and the mortifications he imposed were all the more humiliating because they were often so whimsical. So also in the matter of obedience, the greatest of all mortifications. He might put his orders in the form of requests, but if any hesitation was shown in carrying out those requests they were pressed harder than ever. Sometimes he seemed quite unreasonable in asking people to do things at inconvenient times, but when he did so, it was with the purpose of perfecting their obedience and, through obedience, their humility. He won men by his charm and he retained their adhesion through affection; there were occasions when he drove them relentlessly. Nevertheless, according to the basic idea of the Oratory, they retained their freedom; the only service demanded was one offered willingly.

Now in 1575 Philip obtained at the same moment his Congregation and his church. The church he obtained, however, was hardly more than the site for one, for the building itself was too small and in too bad a state of repair to be of much use. While the other Fathers were discussing how they might renovate and perhaps enlarge it, Philip reached his own decision. Two months after getting it he gave orders that it be torn down and a new church built — the church which is still popularly known in Rome as the *Chiesa Nuova*.

For this he had practically no money at all — only enthusiasm and an unbounded confidence in God. Bacci tells the famous story of how when the demolition was complete and the architect, Matteo di Castello — who had given his services free — was about to mark out the lines of the new building, Philip, who was just then about to say Mass, sent him word to wait until he could come. Then after the architect had drawn the line as far as he considered it ought to go, Philip said, "No, go on further." Three times Philip made him go on before saying, "Now stop and dig." At that point the workmen found an old wall under the ground which not only served as a foundation but supplied a good deal of the materials for the building. Bacci thinks there was something miraculous in this, but be that as it may, at least it justified Philip in wanting what others thought to be an extravagantly large church.

One feels a little sceptical, however, in reading that, "as is generally the case with every work of God, opposition did not fail to arise." For Bacci himself goes on to tell us — with obvious exaggeration — that there was hardly a person in Rome who did not contribute something to the funds that were needed. No very sufficient reason is advanced for the opposition he records, but he says that some people in the neighborhood actually shot with crossbows at Father Lucci while he was supervising the building operations. Though it may be true that "it was observed that all those who had most actively opposed the work died within two years," this would have been more striking had they died within two weeks. The same thing was suggested of the sudden death of Cardinal Rosario in 1559, upon which Cardinal Capecelatro sensibly comments: "Good men of those times were disposed to regard as punishment of crime any visitations of the purely natural order." There is no need to embellish the many instances of the supernatural in the life of Philip Neri with superstitious suppositions.

What is much more to the point is that Philip impulsively began to build with no funds at his disposal and also without ever asking anybody for a single scudo. The first contribution was made by Charles Borromeo who came forward with two hundred crowns — not very much from such a wealthy man, but he could plead that he needed what money he had for his own projects. Gregory XIII made a gift of eight thousand crowns, and an equal amount was contributed by Cardinal Cesi, while his brother Angelo, the

Bishop of Todi, spent at one time and another no less than thirty-six thousand crowns on the "New Church."[2] These and others of the large donations did not all come together, but at least they were made with sufficient regularity to enable the putting up of the church to go forward without interruption for lack of money. The greater part of the necessary funds was supplied by quite poor people in small amounts. All of which shows that Philip not only had powerful and wealthy friends but was generally revered by the populace.

In spite of this there came a time when the lay-brother of the Congregation who was looking after the construction had to tell Philip that the money was about exhausted and that he should ask a certain rich man for help, which he felt sure would not be refused. Philip's answer was, "My son, I have never yet asked anything, and God has always provided for me; that gentleman knows our necessity very well, and if he wishes to give us a contribution he will do it of his own accord." That particular man never did give anything, but a month or two later a distinguished lawyer left four thousand crowns to the church when he died, and six months later another benefactor left double that amount. The new church was not only built but was completed free of debt.

That Philip had retained his good relations with the Florentines — in spite of his troubles at San Giovanni — is shown by the fact that the first stone of the building was

---

[2] The Cardinal, whose generosity was so great, was trying to outdo the benefactions of the Farnese to the Jesuit Church of the Gesù. He was not altogether disinterested and tied strings to his gifts, among them the provision that all ecclesiastics of his family should be regarded as honorary members of the Congregation, with the right to intervene in its affairs. If this right does not appear to have been asserted, it may be because the Cesi brothers never carried out all their promises.

laid by Alessandro de' Medici, the Archbishop of Florence, who also said the first Mass in it. In the days when he was merely the Ambassador of Florence, Philip once said to him, "Well, Alessandro, you will be a cardinal and pope in the end — but you won't last long." When he was elected as Leo XI ten years after Philip's death, he remembered what Philip had said and that Philip had, as he believed, the gift of prophecy. Almost his first words were, "We shall not give you much trouble, for we shall not last long." His was a pontificate of just twenty-five days.

Not only a church was needed but a house for the Fathers. The church itself was used for the Oratory meetings, at such times being closed to all women. The housing problem was a considerable one, for as we are told by Bacci that there were about a hundred and thirty members of the Congregation in 1577, we may suppose that there must have been at least a hundred two years earlier. However, it must be remembered that all the Fathers were not in one place, even then, and that Bacci probably included in his figures the boys' school by then attached to the Congregation. Furthermore, Bacci, of course, includes lay brothers and those who were studying for the priesthood. We know from the many references to the lack of formed men that the number of priests ready for service could not have been large.

This did not alter the fact that a sizeable body of men had to have room found for them, and that there was not enough room in the house. Accordingly some of the Fathers started negotiations to buy the neighboring St. Elizabeth's Convent, which was being given up by the Poor Clares because they were moving elsewhere. As Philip was against making this purchase, saying that he was sure that God would provide for them in some other way, the Fathers acted behind his back, feeling that necessity justified them.

They naturally supposed that the bank bill they were going
to offer would be accepted, as was usual in cases of this sort,
especially as the nuns who were the owners of the property
were satisfied. It was the ecclesiastical dignitary who was
acting for them who insisted on hard cash, so that the whole
affair broke down. When Philip was told of it he said, "Did
I not tell you that the convent was not to be bought? Give
me that bill! God will take care of us." That he knew in
advance of what was afoot Bacci takes to be a striking instance of his prophetic powers; another explanation may be
that the transaction had come to Philip's ears through ordinary channels. After all, he did have many friends in the
banks who could have given him the necessary information.

What is surprising is that even after he had established
his Congregation at the Vallicella, he himself continued to
live at San Girolamo. He had never lived at San Giovanni,
though he had been its rector for thirteen years. The reasons
for this were that he was attached to his old quarters in the
former Franciscan monastery and that he shrank from seeming to acknowledge, by dwelling among his disciples, that
he was actually their superior. The second reason was much
more important than the first, but the first had its weight,
as also had his wish to live an independent rather than a
community life. From 1564 to 1577 those associated with
him had patiently put up with this, though it had involved
a good deal of inconvenience for them. Even in good weather
they lost a lot of time in walking three times a day from
San Giovanni to San Girolamo and back; the only advantage
was that it gave them some exercise which otherwise they
might not have taken. But in bad weather it was a definite
hardship for them that Philip lived elsewhere and that they
had to go to him. There were many occasions when he had
to be consulted and was not at hand. Then again there had

to be a walk to San Girolamo. Men as busy as they were did not see much point in the arrangement.

They had tolerated his whim for thirteen years; now they expected that, as they had their own house, he would join them there. He did nothing of the kind; he announced that he was going to remain where he was. If he had not wanted to appear openly as the rector of San Giovanni, he wanted still less to appear as the founder and superior-general of a new congregation. The more he could keep out of sight the better; at any rate, the better for him. He probably thought it was also better for them; if they were inconvenienced that would be a useful mortification. Not until the end of 1583, over six years after the opening of the Vallicella, did Philip go to live there; and he did so then only at the order of the Pope.

Just as characteristic of him was that he should advance very slowly with the drawing up of the rules, which were not written at all until 1583 and then were regarded as being only tentative. This, of course, had been allowed for in the Pope's Bull, drawn up after consultation with Philip and embodying Philip's own wishes. Instead of having a cut-and-dried scheme from the outset, the idea was that the Fathers of the Congregation at the Vallicella should go on in much the same way as those who had been living at San Giovanni, and that they should develop their rule by degrees, guided by what experience showed them to be advisable. When the first draft of the Constitutions was made in Latin by Bordini in 1583 Philip wrote his famous annotation against the paragraph referring to the individual's ownership of property: "Let him have it and keep it, only let there be no litigation." There was not only to be no vow of poverty, there was not even to be any pooling of the funds. This document is still preserved, as is a draft in

Italian, which also has annotations clearly inspired by Philip though not in his script. The definitive Constitutions were not drawn up until 1612, seventeen years after Philip's death. But that it was his spirit that breathed in them comes out in the Preamble as it finally appeared: "The Congregation of the Oratory was rather moulded and compacted by the example of St. Philip Neri, than governed by laws and rules. He had not, as other religious founders have, a special rule which served him as a guide and appeal. . . . He approved and confirmed, as coming from the Spirit of the Lord, all that his daily experience showed him to be suitable. . . . Hence he was wont to say that he was not in any sense the founder of the Congregation, but that it had been formed and brought to perfection by the great and merciful God Himself. Here then is a brief summary of such observances as he himself established, and of those customs which by his institution have always been received by the members of his Congregation." All this, however, came only after several abortive attempts made by a party within the Congregation to turn it into something more closely resembling a religious order than Philip had in mind. Therefore it was enacted that should any group seek to impose vows, and succeed in obtaining a majority, the minority, however small it might be, was to be regarded as the true Congregation with all its legal and property rights, and the majority, however large, to have cut itself off. Nothing could have been more emphatic.

The long chapter on the founding of the Congregation in Ponnelle and Bordet's study is not only exhaustive but a little exhausting as well. It marks the point where the Abbé Bordet took over the completion of his friend's book, and though he no doubt used Ponnelle's notes to supplement his own researches, he could not take over all his friend's vivacity and charm. What he writes, however, is indispensable to one who would understand the history of the Congregation; the matter need be touched on only briefly in a book which is no more than a personal sketch of Philip Neri. Therefore there is no need to say more here than that the rules as eventually approved merely defined a little more sharply what had been the practice of Philip and his disciples before the Congregation had been so much as thought of. That broad fact seized, the details are of little importance except to the specialist.

One peculiar detail in the rule was that about having at the end of the meal a discussion of two "doubts," as they were called — that is, of two debatable questions, one in moral theology and the other in scripture, each Father speaking briefly in his turn and the proposer of the doubt making a summing-up at the end. From 1564, when the first Fathers moved to San Giovanni, these little debates had been their custom, the only difference between that time and later being that at first only one such point was discussed instead of two. While this is not a very startling departure from the ordinary usage of public reading or sermons in community refectories, it is at all events unique. Whatever other departures were introduced were equally slight, with the exception of the novel idea — novel at least as worked out — of a community life without vows.

This central idea was not always clearly perceived even by those closest to Philip, or when perceived, was not always recognised as of the essence of the Oratory. There was a party which took the existing rules only as something providing for an interim stage and which was confident that the Oratory would (and should) develop into a religious order. Philip's age was one of drastic ecclesiastical reform, and virtually all the new religious institutes that arose during the sixteenth and seventeenth centuries had as at least one of their declared purposes the renovation of the secular clergy. Thus on October 8, 1579, we find Tarugi writing to St. Charles Borromeo begging him to use his influence with the Pope to get the Congregation transformed into a "seminary of secular subjects who could be scattered throughout the world to assist the bishops." Talpa also had this idea of the Congregation being used as the instrument of a universal reform of the secular clergy. It was something often pressed upon Philip by his most prominent associates — Baronius being one of the few exceptions. But excellent as this idea was in itself, nothing could have been further from Philip's mind. He knew what he wanted and that the grandiose schemes of Talpa and Tarugi were at complete variance with the Oratory as he conceived it. They believed that it was possible to combine the distinctive work of the exercises with the work of a more extensive character, and they were probably correct in holding that such a declared purpose would attract many men to the Congregation. In spite of this, Philip held fast to his original notion and would never allow anything to interfere with it. Only with the greatest reluctance did he permit even the founding of a few houses outside of Rome, and then only because he could hardly help this happening. As Pastor notes: "The spreading of his Congregation after the manner of the great Orders had no place in Philip's intentions." His humility — the humility that had so long resisted the founding of the Congregation at all — forbade his making it appear as a rival to, say, the Society of Jesus. His good sense also operated; he understood that the direction of a widespread organization did not come within the scope of his special talents. What he could do, that he did — a work in which everything depended upon a direct personal intercourse between his disciples and himself. He therefore ended in all essentials as he had begun — as a hearer of confessions and the promoter of intimate conferences that supplemented the confessional. He was from start to finish a director of souls; he never wanted to be anything else.

The originality of the Oratory, as Talpa truly pointed out, "consists principally in the daily use of the Word of God, in a simple, familiar and efficacious manner, and very different from the usual style of preachers . . . [Philip] intended our distinctive and special exercise, the exercise by which we are different from other Institutes, to be the Word of God, and not merely the Word of God in itself, but the Word of God preached daily in a familiar way." Tarugi added, "The idea of our founder was that the Institute should have for its special and proper function the preaching of the Word of God on every day of the week, as well as on Sundays." But they might have added still further that this preaching was designed to bring about an intimate relationship between the Fathers and those who frequented the Oratory and that it was not intended to end with the delivery of the sermons. It was a means of giving the penitents of the Oratory the instructions and exhortations for which there was no time in the confessional itself; it was thought of by Philip as supplementary to his prime instrument of the confessional.

Everything else was subsidiary. How much this was so appears in the fact that in the activities even of the Confraternity of Pilgrims and Convalescents, founded by Philip to provide for the jubilee of 1550, he took little or no part at the time of the next jubilee twenty-five years later. He had done what needed to be done in initiating that work; he now left it to forge ahead on its own steam. People, however, did not forget to whom it owed its origin, which was another reason why Philip wished to keep his own name out of the matter. In case the credit should be pressed upon him, he was careful not to appear as more than an honorary member of the Confraternity. But most of all he wished to reserve all his time and energy for the Oratory.

All this was something not very perfectly realised by his great friend Cardinal Charles Borromeo. We have seen how from 1566 — if not before — he had tried to get Philip to send him men and had even, at one period during the reign of Pius V, come near to succeeding in inducing Philip to transfer himself and his activities to Milan. Now that he was back in Rome for the Jubilee of 1575 he renewed his pleas, being "a most rapacious robber, who always carries off the best," as Philip put it. And Charles would have carried off the best, had Philip permitted him to do so. Especially had the Cardinal-Archbishop set his heart on obtaining the services of Baronius and Tarugi and Talpa; and what is more, Tarugi and Talpa — who had always been leaders of the party that tried to convince Philip that he should become a leader of reform — were perfectly willing to go. But Philip was more than a match for Charles; though he gave him two and afterwards another two priests to start an Oratory at Milan, Baronius and Talpa and Tarugi were not among them.

Nor was the Cardinal-Archbishop allowed to keep even these very long. From the outset there were difficulties. St. Charles would consent to their saying Mass according to the Roman rite only for so long as was needed for them to familiarise themselves with the Ambrosian rite generally used in his diocese. The meaning of this did not escape Philip. As there were churches in Milan in which the Roman rite was used, there would have been nothing anomalous in permitting this to the Oratorians. St. Charles's action indicated that he proposed to absorb them completely.

He was ready enough — indeed, he was anxious — that they should establish an Oratory there on the Roman model. But his main idea was to employ them in a capacity that would have made them virtually his vicars-general; they were to help him administer his diocese. And he would not take no for an answer. About this he was perfectly explicit. Writing to Speciano, he said: "I see that the ideas of these Fathers do not at all agree with mine. They want their congregation to depend on themselves alone, and I want everything to depend on me; it being my object to have a body of men, formed indeed as priests of the Oratory, but ready to obey every intimation of my will."

Left to themselves they would probably have acquiesced, for it was evident that there was much good that they could do in Milan. The trouble was that it was not their own distinctive work that St. Charles was calling on them to perform. Therefore in July, 1576, Philip suddenly acted with the ruthless decision he could display at times, and instructed Tarugi — the main advocate of the Milan project — "Write in my name to the Fathers at Milan, that on receipt of your letter, they must immediately and without a moment's delay return to Rome." Tarugi argued in vain. Philip was adamant and would not allow even a brief respite, as he knew that this would certainly lead to other delays while negotiations for a compromise were started. Tarugi must write at once, and the four Fathers at Milan must return at once. Well might Charles describe Philip as a man without mercy.

Yet Philip's action made no difference to the cordial relations between himself and Charles. When the Cardinal was

in Rome again in 1579 he not only spent as much time with
Philip as he could but adopted toward him the reverent
attitude of a disciple. If the priest was now over sixty,
Charles was forty-one, and the former disparity of age had
diminished. In any event, his exalted position in the Church
and the rank of his family had always been much more than
enough to offset this. But though Philip treated him with all
deference, he was outdone by the Cardinal-Archbishop who,
after they had said Office or had prayed together, would
kneel and in tears kiss Philip's hand.

There was a final misunderstanding in 1581. Charles managed to get Philip to promise two priests for William V, the
Duke of Bavaria, who was zealously promoting the Catholic
cause in Germany. Upon this Speciano, going directly to
the Pope, got him to appoint two Oratorian Fathers, one of
them Bordini. Philip in his turn went to the Pope, explaining that he could not spare these men; but he found two
others, who had no connection with his Congregation, who
said they were willing to go. Then they withdrew, and
Charles Borromeo was very angry and accused Philip of
breaking his promises. This, however, Philip had not done;
the two men who had backed down were not his subjects,
as he pointed out in a letter to Charles. But before he was
able to write that calm letter he wrote another, which was
not sent. In it he gave vent to his own indignation. The
original letter — whose many corrections and erasures reveal the agitation in which he wrote — may be seen at the
Vallicella. Ponnelle comments: "This dispute reflects dis-
credit on neither of the antagonists, but it throws their characters into strong relief; that of St. Charles rather cold and
authoritative, and that of Philip subject to the extremity
of emotion and only calmed by degrees as the result of his
humility and his goodness."

By now St. Charles had founded his own Congregation of St. Ambrose, as he had failed to obtain Philip's assistance. And he consulted Philip about the drawing up of its rules. Philip always managed to find a pretext for not giving his opinion, and the story is that one day when the Cardinal took him for a drive in his carriage, Philip suggested that they should call on the Capuchins at San Bonaventura. Charles naturally supposed that the intention was to take him to some expert on canon law; instead Philip asked for the lay-brother Felice da Cantalice.

Fra Felice was a well-known character on the streets of Rome — almost as well-known there as Philip himself. Doing nothing but beg for his convent and saying nothing but *Deo gratias* whether he got an alms or not, he was commonly known as Brother Deo Gratias. By such simplicity he had achieved sanctity and was eventually to be canonized. St. Charles, however, must have been astonished when a man who could neither read nor write was brought in to advise him, and Philip no doubt enjoyed the humor of the situation — the Cardinal's eyebrows lifted, the poor lay-brother covered with confusion and perhaps suspecting another of Philip's practical jokes. But Philip had, as was invariably the case with him, sound sense under his whimsicality. Put under obedience, Brother Felice gave his opinion — that of a saint, if an illiterate man — with the consequence that the rules read to him were amended in accordance with his suggestions.

There we have Philip's method — something always direct and personal. We have to reject as a piece of pure fiction — because it is so completely at variance with all that we know of him — the scheme attributed to him in a document written several years after his death and quoted by the Abbé Ponnelle. It was that of bringing about "reform in the Church by means of Rome, in Rome by means of the Curia, in the Curia by means of the clergy, and in the clergy by means of the Congregation." Such a beautifully logical plan of campaign was of the kind that it would not have needed much encouragement to make Talpa adopt; it was precisely the kind of thing that the modesty of Philip most shrank from.

Nevertheless, he did have a great deal to do with the reform of the Church; but he was all the more effectual in that he stood almost alone during that time of centralization and efficiency for doing things on the spur of the moment, in acting from day to day by happy inspiration without any thought of the morrow and without any settled policy. His unconventional and haphazard ways had often brought him under suspicion during the earlier years of his priesthood, but they were his means of reaching those for whom he had established his apostolate. Just because he did not set out to "influence" people — except in the sense of making them better Christians — his influence, especially towards the end of his life, was enormous. But even with the series of Popes who were his friends he never sought to promote any projects, with one solitary exception which will be mentioned later. Apart from this, his effect upon the Church was that of his personal sanctity.

But it should be added that he could not have achieved what he did had he not lived at the centre of Christendom. Gregory XIII had been thinking mainly of the convenience of the courtiers when he had urged Philip to settle at the Vallicella. The selection of that centre proved to be providential. For so many courtiers went there that during Philip's later years they formed the majority of those who attended the exercises at the Oratory. Therefore through them Philip's influence radiated out in every direction; and these were the very men by whose means the reform of the Church was so largely brought about. It is understandable that some of Philip's brilliant and energetic followers should have tried to force the role of reformer upon him. It is clear, from our vantage-point in history, that he was right in refusing that role. Here his instinct, which so often seemed capricious and even stubborn, was profoundly wise. It was as an individualist, a free-lance, that he was to make his great contribution to reform. We can never be sufficiently grateful to such men as Ignatius and Pius V and Charles Borromeo; it was fortunate for the Church that, side by side with them, there was the eccentric Philip Neri, unconventional, unpredictable, but moved always by the inspiration of the Holy Ghost.

Chapter Ten

ALL THINGS TO ALL MEN

PHILIP was one of those quick-witted and vivacious people who are interested in everything and can talk about anything. Especially at his first encounter with a man, he would draw him out by "talking shop," knowing that, contrary to the prevailing opinion, shop is always a fascinating subject. A lawyer wondered how this old priest with the small bright blue eyes could know so much about law; but he wondered no more than did doctors or bankers or poets when they discovered how much Father Philip knew about their line of work. The explanation of course is that he learned what he did by talking to other doctors and bankers and poets. He had never specialized in anything except life, and though there he stressed the spiritual life, he was able to relate all human activities to his one great aim.

It was not that he deliberately spread the nets of his personal charm; he was much too natural for that. But it was certainly his personal charm that proved to be in the majority of instances the basis of the initial attraction he had for so many totally different types of people. All instantly felt his warm sympathy. He did not have to "work up" an interest in the men and women he met; it flowed out spontaneously. He drew the world to him by his inexhaustible capacity for affection.

By now it should be apparent that, though it was his habit to speak and act without premeditation, he was not quite without system. He was, however, not attached to system as such. As Father Matthews of the London Oratory writes in his little book: "His method was, in effect, to have no standardized method. He acted from day to day and from hour to hour according to the impulses of tender charity to treat one soul in this way and another in that, in obedience to the interior movements of the Holy Spirit, whose guidance he so humbly and constantly sought and so faithfully tried to follow. He won souls partly by his personal charm, partly by the exercise of supernatural gifts. He prayed and trembled and wept; he read comic books and went in ecstasies; he caressed young men and boxed their ears to make them cheerful; he made jokes and told men their sins before they confessed them; but there were few who could resist the charm of Philip's personality and the vehemence of his prayers combined."

As an individualist, he had developed the bent of his natural character — mercilessly mortifying, indeed, the baser instincts that were in him, as they are in all men, and doing this so thoroughly that we never once catch the slightest glimpse of them. Yet this suppression of evil was the only way of truly developing himself; only in this way could the best in him have a chance to flower without being choked with weeds. In the same way he encouraged his disciples to be themselves. Though he felt uneasy about them whenever they were too long a time out of his sight, and though he made them very dependent upon him, he was careful not to attempt to mould them all into one pattern. One of the principles he instilled into the Fathers of the Congregation was that they were not to try to impose their own spiritual methods upon their penitents, as what might be excellent in one case might not be at all suitable in another. He found a natural as well as a supernatural pleasure in the fact that human beings are so different from one another. But he knew that nobody can be fully himself unless he has surrendered to God.

All the same he did not expect too much. It was enough, he used to say, if a man at the beginning of his conversion can be kept from mortal sin. He was against anyone attempting more than he could perform; a little done well was much to be preferred to tasks that were so heavy as to be likely to end in discouragement. Even while pointing his followers to the heights, he realised that many would not succeed in climbing very far and so adjusted the pace to the individual capacity. Each case was unique and had to be handled in a special way.

This was why he laid such an emphasis on frequent confession. Many of his disciples confessed themselves every day, and the rule in the Congregation was that every man should make his confession at least three times every week. But this by no means implied that all were encouraged to go to Communion every day. Philip would not even let all his priests say Mass every day, though they were expected to be prepared to say Mass whenever he told them to do so. At the beginning he may have been to some extent Cacciaguerra's disciple, but not for long. While he did of course promote frequent Communion, and never held anybody back because of anything even faintly suggesting Jansenistic scruples, he was more concerned about confession than Communion. For confession was his means of directing his followers in their spiritual life. The Abbé Bordet writes: "In the spirituality of Philip we meet then with these two extremes: the most minute control of the interior life, and the most complete spontaneity."

He never gave the world any spiritual treatises, though he was deeply to influence those who did, especially St. Francis de Sales. For that matter, Philip had the greatest disinclination for writing so much as a letter, and though one of his best portraits shows him with a pen in his hand, it was a pen that was rarely used. He might improvise a sonnet now and then; he was constitutionally unable to sit long at his desk.[1] Because of his lack of appetite for authorship, we are left with hardly more than such of his maxims as his disciples remembered. From these emerge two things as of universal application: he insisted upon humility, and he insisted upon cheerfulness.

He did not of course expect everybody to exhibit his own special brand of gaiety, and nobody else did, though many of the men around him were high-spirited and vivacious. But he was convinced that the gloomy could make no advance in the spiritual life. "I want you never to commit sin," he used to tell them, "but to be always gay and cheerful of heart." One of his favorite sayings was, "A cheerful and glad spirit attains to perfection much more readily than a melancholy spirit." He liked people to laugh and joke — was he not always laughing and joking himself? — and a blithe heart was to him a sign of innocence.

Merely to look at his shining eyes was enough to cure the depression that comes over most men at times. It was impossible not to be cheerful in his good company. There were those who found their weight of cares or their tempera-

---

[1] A few days before his death, as he knew he was about to die, he destroyed all his papers he could lay hands on. A few letters, because they were in the possession of other people, escaped; but there had never been very many of them. As for his poems, though we have a few scraps of his improvised verse, only one sonnet remains of which we can be sure that it was by him. The others formerly attributed to him are not by him at all. We know, however, that in his youth he had written a good deal of verse and that he continued to do so occasionally all his life.

mental melancholy lifted as they walked down the corri-
dor towards the room of the happy saint. Some, when they
did not find him there, were cheered up simply by going in
and staying a few minutes. Fabrizio de' Massimi found it
sufficed just to stand outside the door. "Philip's room," his
young men often said, "is not a room but a paradise."

There are some forms of human frailty which produce a
species of joy — false though it is and leading to bitterness
— yet by this very fact show that they must be much less
reprehensible than the dullness of avarice or the devas-
tating loneliness of pride. Rightly did Dante clothe the
hypocrites in hell with mantles of lead. Similarly Philip was
accustomed to say, "He who is in any degree possessed by
avarice will never make any progress in virtue. . . . It is far
easier to convert to God the sensual than the covetous."
Joy, even when not to Philip a mark of holiness, was one of
the swiftest of roads to holiness. Knowing as he did that
most unhappiness is caused by self-love and that egotists are
invariably miserable, he made it his main business to bring
people to humility. These are the twin points of his body
of doctrine, in so far as he can be said to have had one.

Of these two points much the more important of course
was humility. For he knew that from humility joy would be
sure to flow. Even a psychology unillumined by grace has
perceived that the more completely a man is detached the
greater will be his happiness, and that man's good does not
consist in increasing the number of his wants but in di-
minishing them. In order to bring about that detachment,
and to foster humility, it was Philip's custom to subject
his penitents to extraordinary mortifications. These were
virtually never mortifications of a bodily sort, for though
he practiced such mortifications himself and though the
brothers of the Oratory took the discipline in common three

times a week, Philip laid almost his entire stress upon mortifications that were interior, mortifications of the will. The
whole of a man's sanctity, he used to say, lies within the
compass of three fingers laid on his forehead, for it was
there that a rebellious judgment resisted the operations of
grace. Quoting St. Bernard's *Sperne mundum, sperne seip-
sum, sperne nullum, sperne se sperni,* he went to almost
fantastic lengths in teaching his disciples to despise the
opinion others might have of them. In this respect Cardinal
Capecelatro, who was one of his sons, writes, "In all else he
was ineffably gentle; in this alone he seemed at times almost
harsh, unjust and without pity." It was the very essence of
his asceticism, and in this he gave an example and outdid
everybody else. He did not expect other people to fast as
he did; on the contrary, he encouraged the Dominican novices to eat and grow fat and warned his followers against
the danger of undermining their constitution by excessive
austerities. What he did expect was that they should be
willing to make fools of themselves, if he told them to do so.
He often did just that, yet apparently they always accepted
this kind of mortification.

It is probable, however, that these methods tended to
lose their effectiveness. For the same reason that people
came to have all the higher opinion of Philip as soon as they
discovered that his antics had the purpose of lessening men's
esteem for him, they also ceased jeering at his disciples
when they were seen doing something ridiculous. At first
there was loud laughter in the streets when one of his fine
young gentlemen walked along carrying his dog Capriccio,
or dressed in satin was sweeping the church porch; in the
end these actions elicited admiration. And if Philip afterwards used the cat he had left behind at San Girolamo in
the same way, sending this or that of his disciples to feed

her, and then inquiring on his return — with minute particularity, if some person of dignity happened to be present — how the dear little animal was, that also evoked edification rather than jeering. Those present might be amused; they were also impressed; they might even feel a little awed.

It was the same when young Antonio Gallonio appeared for a theological examination at which the Pope himself was present. When the answer was given that there was no need to question so learned a man, everybody smiled of course; but everybody also understood that Gallonio spoke with such seeming arrogance only because he was humbly following Philip's instructions. And when Gallonio, who had incautiously let it out that he knew some comic songs in patois, was made to sing them whenever cardinals or nuns happened to be present, that, too, provided edification as well as entertainment — though perhaps in this instance Philip wished to mortify the audience as well as the performer. He was obliged to be very fertile and ingenious in inventing new mortifications to have this method succeed at all.

But if Philip often appeared to be hard on his disciples, they all knew that, along with this severity of his, went a vast tenderness. The Barnabite Tito degli Alessi, who was living at San Girolamo in 1574, wrote in a letter that all the priests of the Congregation "show him great submission and reverence, even though he sometimes gives them some good mortifications; but he has a way of inflicting blows that do not seem to wound." That was Philip's secret. If he punished the good, he treated sinners with the utmost kindness. To be treated severely was a sign that one was advancing in the spiritual life.

This kindness of Philip's always came out in confession. Then if his penitents were shamefaced in revealing their sins, he was very likely to do it for them. And while he was pronouncing the words of absolution he would hold them to his breast, in which they could feel his heart beating like a hammer.

In the case of women he was inclined to be a bit brusque. In the early years of his priesthood, while he could not of course refuse to hear their confessions, he avoided even that as far as possible, and when they did go to him he quickly dismissed them. But when he became old he permitted himself to be more fatherly and would sometimes place his hand on their heads as he absolved them. Now and then, too, he even used a little humor, as in the case of the young widow who confessed to Father Angelo Velli that she found it difficult to rid herself of her sensual temptations. Sent to Philip, she was told, "When you feel temptations of this sort, just say to the devil, 'I will accuse you to that dull ass of a Philip.'" The strange method worked wonderfully well.

What is more remarkable, however, is that Philip seemed to know what were the sins of those who went to confession to him even before they accused themselves. While it need not be supposed that this always happened, it happened very often. Time after time witnesses at the Process for his beatification testified most explicitly to the fact that he knew in advance all about them. And if generally he showed this knowledge by being able to tell them their sins, there was at least one case — that of Raffaello Lupo, a young man whom an officious friend more or less tricked into going to confession to Philip, and who therefore invented a catalogue of sins on the spur of the moment — when Philip at the end of the confession said mildly, "The Holy Ghost has revealed to me that there is not a word of truth in all that you have told me."

Then there was the youth of sixteen who had been ordained priest at the instance of his family in order to qual-

ify himself for a rich benefice. Having obtained it, he made
no pretence of living as a priest and continued to dress
like a layman. Philip asked him at once, "Aren't you a
priest?" He admitted that he was and asked Philip how he
knew. The answer came, "Because of the radiance around
your head." It was certainly not the radiance of sanctity,
but Philip was at once conscious of his sacerdotal character.

This sort of thing may perhaps be sometimes accounted
for, the Abbé Ponnelle suggests, on the ground of profes-
sional experience. But it certainly cannot always be accounted for on that ground, for we hear of such incidents
very soon after Philip's ordination, at a time before he could
have gained much experience in the confessional. To take
the case of the young cleric just mentioned — Tomaso da San
Geminiano — had he lived as a priest for some years, he
might have been recognisable by a sharp eye even in disguise, for the sacerdotal mode of life puts its mark on a man.
That Philip picked him out at once indicates some other
sort of insight.

Yet it may be supposed that Philip was by nature hyper-
sensitive; his telepathic powers and his gift of second sight,
if so one would view them, need not be regarded as supernatural, however much his natural gifts had been height-
ened by the supernatural life he was living. But there are
occasions when such an explanation does not quite suffice.
Thus Cardinal Federigo Borromeo testified under oath that
in confession Philip said to him: "Do not doubt that I have
seen your state and the needs of your soul. You must know
that God has revealed it to me, and has shown me many
things; I tell you that I have had a revelation about it. Ah,
if you only knew what I have seen!" And even when natural explanations can be offered, it is clear that those who

knew of Philip's powers considered them to be supernatural and were drawn to him as a confessor on that account.

It might sometimes appear as though Philip was almost a little morbid in his insistence upon frequent and even daily confession. It can hardly be that he expected his disciples to commit mortal sins every day. The explanation of course is that Philip used the confessional as a means of directing their spiritual lives and of uprooting the smaller imperfections which, if neglected, can lead to great sins. As Tarugi wrote in 1579: "The spirit of the Congregation is not to restrict [the sacrament of penance] to confession of sins alone, but to make use of it to encourage penitents in the way of well-doing and to urge them forward continually, while always keeping them under the care and discipline of their confessors." Through the confessional Philip bound his disciples to himself, and grace came to them by means of the sacrament. The act of confession secured the all-important humility at which he aimed. This applied specially to the members of his Congregation; until shortly before his death he was confessor to the whole community, hearing each man's confession at least three times a week. Because of this no founder of a religious institute has ever had so intimate a relationship with his subjects; Philip was the soul of everything that was done at the Oratory.

In addition to the Fathers and the lay-brothers he still had a large number of laymen whose confessions he heard equally often. He was available to them at all hours of the day and night, and he had his own methods for making sure that they would go to see him regularly. Thus he accepted a couple of song-birds from Louis Ames, the Frenchman attached to the custom-house whom he had known since his early days in Rome. But in accepting them he stipulated that Ames should come every day to look after them, and he had similar devices for making sure that other men should visit him frequently. One day Ames arrived to find the cage open and one of the birds flying around Philip's face singing all the time. However often it was driven away it would always come back, flying from his feet up to his head. Marvelling at the sight, Ames must have seen in this something not unlike Philip's power to attract men.

If in many of the reports left of his behavior and speech — his thumping people on the back, or pulling their hair or ears, or taking hold of them by the chin, or addressing them as "idiot" or "animal" — he strikes us as a bit rough, it is clear that, so far from resenting his familiar ways, people loved him all the more on this account. And we must remember that, while such things were considered sufficiently unusual to excite comment, the Italian manners of the time were very free.

He sometimes used his methods, slightly modified, in the confessional, and even with women. Thus Sulpitia Sirleta, noticing his peculiar way of saying Mass — his violent tremblings, his sighs, his gestures, and his feet that now seemed to be dancing and then actually lifted into the air — thought to herself, "That man is possessed!" Then feeling that she had sinned by making so rash a judgment, she went to confess to Philip, very much embarrassed by what she had to tell. She showed such difficulty in getting it out that Philip had to go to her rescue. "Come, come, you silly creature," he said; "you have been finding fault with me, haven't you?" She admitted that she had. "Well, what did you say?" "Father," she explained, "I saw you raised from the ground while you were saying Mass." At once he replied, "Hold your tongue! Hold your tongue!" She told him that this was what had made her think him possessed, at which he laughed heartily and said, "It is true, it is true. I *am* possessed."

In a similar off-hand way he dealt with Sister Scholastica, a nun at Santa Marta. She was going to confess to him a temptation she had never mentioned before — a temptation to despair of her salvation. She had brought herself close to believing that she would be lost. Philip struck first. "What are you doing, Scolastica, what are you doing?" — this was a phrase always on his lips — "Paradise is yours." She returned despondently, "No, Father; I am afraid it is not so and that I shall be lost." "All right," Philip said, "I'll prove it to you that you won't be. Tell me, for whom did Christ die?" "For sinners." "And what are you?" "A sinner." "Then," he told her, "Paradise is yours, because you repent of your sins." She never again experienced her temptation to despair.

All Philip's dealings with his disciples had as their object the kindling of fervor. That was what he sought in the afternoon exercises at the Oratory; still more was it aimed at the evening sessions of prayer. Nobody could have ever acquired what amounted to a habit of fervor more completely than Philip himself. His face and his shaking body revealed it and imparted it to others. The form of prayer — that of silent meditation followed by the saying of the litanies — was chosen rather than the divine office because, as Capecelatro points out, "he wished to unite in it priests and men of the world." Yet Philip would presumably not have denied that participation in the liturgy is, even for the laity, to be preferred ordinarily to all other kinds of prayer; but however fully he might have admitted this in the abstract, he saw that the kind of prayer practiced at the Oratory was better for his immediate purpose. It did not prevent him from frequently taking a select group of his laymen into the choir of the Minerva to sing Vespers or Compline with the friars.

What must be remembered is that at this time monasticism was suffering a temporary decline. Though monks abounded, their wealth had brought about the obnoxious system of commendatory abbots — men who did nothing for the abbey but were handsomely provided for out of its revenues. It was inevitable that such a state of affairs resulted in slackness and sloth and that the performance of the *Opus Dei* should have come to be regarded as something of an anachronism. All the new orders and congregations dropped it, so Philip was by no means alone in this. What can be said of him was that he at least remained considerably closer to the older tradition of spirituality than most of his reforming contemporaries.

It is significant that the favorite books at the Oratory for public use were the *laudi* of Jacopone da Todi, which were sung whenever possible, but which also often formed the basis of commentary, and the anonymous Life of St. Colombini of Siena, who was then only one of the *Beati*. A good deal of light is thrown on the spirit of Philip's institute, and even its psychological methods, by the following passage from that biography. Colombini saw three main means of increasing love for Christ. The first was to speak constantly of Him. The second was to cultivate charity towards all God's creatures. The third was to practice mortification.

Here was almost the whole program of the Oratory. And the Philippine conviction that "the more strongly a man speaks, the more he feels," that emotion is induced by action, suggests a modern pragmatist. Colombini is quoted by his biographer as having said: "It is my opinion that virtues are failing because we fail to speak enough of God, for I have seen and known that, as a natural consequence, the heart feels what the tongue utters; so that he whose talk is of the world grows lukewarm and worldly; he who speaks

of Christ thinks of Christ. Therefore if you wish Christ to
give Himself to you, you will always be ready to speak, sing
or read of Christ, or else to meditate on or pray to Him."
Though there is of course another side to that; though there
are those of whom Christ Himself spoke who say, "Lord,
Lord!" and yet will hear on the Judgment Day, "I never
knew you," it must at least be said that there was no place
for such men at the Oratory. There was only passionate
sincerity and the flame of fervor. It may be that Philip's
methods would not have worked so well with races of a
less ardent disposition; there can be no question but that
they were wonderfully well adapted for the Italians for
whom they were designed.

The Italian temperament must, in fact, be allowed for in
much that we hear of in connection with Philip. His appeal
has been of course by no means limited to Italians, for one
of the greatest of his sons is that extremely English Englishman, John Henry Newman. Nevertheless Philip's appeal was
addressed, in the first instance, to men whose blood moved
a good deal more quickly than our own. If there are moments when the atmosphere seems to us a little like that of
a hot-house; if we sometimes encounter what may strike us
as too great a disposition among these people to see the
miraculous in happenings which our calmer (and, it need
hardly be said, superior) judgment cannot bring itself to
believe were miraculous, the advantage is not necessarily all
with us. None of us, let it be hoped, will see the "black dogs"
that so terrified several of Philip's penitents as they lay
dying, and we may not unreasonably hold that these apparitions existed only in tormented imaginations; but to have so
vivid a fear of hell is not a bad thing at all. And Philip always succeeded in bringing these people a peace in which
they could confidently yield their souls to God. Persiano

Rosa, when dying in 1558, himself saw these dogs, and they
had to be driven away by "St. Philip," as Rosa was calling
his former penitent. Surely he may be considered to have
been in better case than those who in their last moments
refuse to trouble themselves about their spiritual condition.
In any event, Italians should not be despised because of the
liveliness of their fancy, or blamed because they do not
have the phlegm of Englishmen.

For the English, it might be recorded, Philip had a special
affection. Their college at Rome, founded by Gregory XIII to
supply priests during the Elizabethan persecution, was situated directly opposite San Girolamo della Carità. In the
street Philip frequently met its students and invariably
greeted them with *Salvete, Flores Martyrum!* According to
tradition, it was their custom upon ordination to go to the
old saint to get his blessing before they left for England.
The tradition continues that all who did this suffered martyrdom, and that the only man who neglected to ask Philip's
blessing eventually apostatised. It goes without saying that
Philip considered that the martyrdom for which these students were preparing themselves was far more to be desired than the most fervent of feelings; but he understood
that the Italian temperament had to be worked upon in this
way. Before we become too critical of Italian emotionalism
and credulity and superstition, we might recall that Italians
have always been too cool-headed to go in for anything
even faintly resembling the hysterical orgies of the Ameri-
can camp-meeting.

For Jews Philip also had a particular fondness. Of these
he converted a good many, never by arguing with them but
by praying for them and inviting them to pray with him to
the God of Abraham, Isaac, and Jacob. Four of these —

brothers — he had pleaded with for a long time with no success, until one evening he announced that at Mass the next morning he was going to do "holy violence" to God on their behalf. Confidently he went on, "Tomorrow during my Mass they will say *yes*." It turned out just as he had prophesied. The four youths were baptised together by Pope Clement VIII. Philip was so delighted with their keen intelligence that he pronounced them four little jewels.

If a few of his converts did not turn out well, that was only to be expected. The remarkable thing is that almost all of them persevered. Of those who did not, the most famous case is that of Giacomo Paleologos, who had been a Dominican and who claimed to be connected with the family of the last Byzantine Emperor. After having taught theology at Bologna he had gone over to the reformers, as had that Bernardino Ochino, whose defection in the late 'thirties had all but ruined the newly-founded Capuchins, of whom he was vicar-general. In 1582, some years after the death of Emperor Maximilian II, who had protected him, Paleologos was handed over to the Roman authorities. Condemned by the Inquisition to be burnt at the stake, he was about to have the execution carried out when Philip intervened. Word was sent to Gregory XIII that a willingness to abjure his heresy had been expressed, so Paleologos — he was probably not a Paleologus at all, his true name being Massigliara — was led back to prison. There Philip did not argue with him — for St. Robert Bellarmine had already done this to no effect — but instead got him to read Colombini and Jacopone da Todi. In the end, however, it all failed. The Inquisition came to doubt the sincerity of his conversion and in 1585 he was condemned again, this time to be beheaded. On the scaffold he once more recanted but too late. Baronius heard his last confession. Philip used to say afterwards, "I was never over pleased with that man's conversion."

Paleologos is remembered as Philip's chief failure because of his celebrity. If there were other failures, it is generally true that, if Philip ever got hold of a man, there was not much likelihood of his falling away; he was too well looked after for that. What happened far more often was that the convert eventually entered religion, for though Philip himself never had had any idea of entering an order, he encouraged his converts to do so. Nearly every week at the Vallicella at least one of those who had been attending came to the front at the end of the meeting to kneel down and ask the prayers of those present for his vocation. Philip's advice in this matter was accepted as that of an oracle. The General of the Barnabites was so impressed by his insight that he told the head of the house in Rome to accept no candidates unless they had been approved by Philip. And at some time during the period when he was General of the Jesuits (1567–1572), it is said that St. Francis Borgia, the Duke of Gandia, the great-grandson of the notorious Alexander VI, tried to get Philip to train the novices of the Society. So the story runs. At all events it was noticed that those whom Philip had advised to enter the cloister persevered, while those whom he tried to dissuade sooner or later left of their own accord. What was also noticed was that in all this Philip showed astonishing self-abnegation. He could have had the pick of the men in Rome for his Congregation, but he never tried to influence their decision in his favor. The only two exceptions were those of Tarugi and Baronius, both of whom had thought of joining the Capuchins; Philip could hardly have been expected to let two such treasures go. Doubtless, however, he was convinced they were in their right place.

One of the most arresting instances of his insight occurred in 1576 when a young man named Girolamo Beger went to the Minerva and told Fra Pietromartire that he felt a strong impulse to be a Dominican. Somewhat at a loss as to what to say, the novice-master suggested that he consult Philip first, which he did that same hour. Philip playfully took hold of a lock of his hair and greeted him with, "I know what you want. Fra Pietromartire has sent you to me to know if you are fit to be a friar. Well now, go, fulfill your desire, and thank God that He has called you to His service." There was no way Philip could have had any intimation of what Beger had come to tell him. One may perhaps account for Philip's knowing of the purpose of the visit by telepathy, and it is possible that Philip had already seen enough of Beger to be impressed by him. The young man, however, naturally took this as a case of divine revelation. In any event the advice was sound: Beger died many years later as Preacher-general of his order.

Against this we may set Bacci's story about Francesco Pucci of Palestrina. He made a vow, in spite of Philip's advice, that he would become a Capuchin, and Philip, who still disapproved, obtained him a papal dispensation. Even after that Francesco's mind was not set at rest. So Philip spoke to the General of the Capuchins about his case. The next time the young man went to see the General, he was asked, "So you have made a vow to join us?" "Yes, Father," was the reply. To this the General said, "Well, *you* may have made a vow to join us but *we* have made no vow to receive you." We may suspect that Philip had a hand in that device for settling Francesco's scruples. His general rule remained that of urging men to make themselves saints while living in the world. In particular he was always reluctant to permit those attached to the court, where they were in a position to do much good and give much edification, to leave it for a monastery.

A large part of Philip's success lay in his making himself available to anybody at any time. This was a cardinal point with him, and if any of the Fathers, seeing that he was tired or knowing that he was busy, tried to spare him by keeping visitors away, he was sure to get a sharp rebuke, if Philip heard of it. "I tell you," he would say, "that those of my penitents who are now most spiritual are the very ones I gained to the Lord by being always accessible, even at night." Night and day he was at anyone's beck and call. He still kept his key under his door, in case a man wanted to come to him in the small hours. He was at the command of all Rome.

With women he was by now much less aloof than he had been during his first years as a priest. Though women were never admitted to the Oratory meetings, or allowed to go on its excursions, they were allowed to attend the outdoor gatherings that were held in fine weather; for it would have been impossible to keep them away from the edge of the crowd. And Philip could not but get intimately acquainted with the wives and feminine relatives of his disciples. His work nevertheless remained one distinctively for men.

If of his extant letters half were addressed to women, this may be because women are more likely than men to preserve letters. It is worthy of note that of these the largest number and the longest letters are those written to Sister Maria Trievi or Tregui, who was a nun at the convent of Santa Lucia in Florence. As might be expected, they are mainly taken up with advice about her spiritual life. But

she was a niece. Another woman who received several letters from him was Fiora Ragni,² and the first of these is
worth quoting in full. It reads: "Although I never write to
anyone, I cannot help doing so to Madonna Fiora, who is
like my first-born daughter, and whom I am very anxious
to see flower: moreover that afterwards the flower may produce good fruit, the fruit of humility, patience, and all
virtues, and that she may be the lodging and vessel of the
Holy Spirit; as indeed is commonly the case of those who
go often to Holy Communion. If this were not so I would
not have you for a daughter; or if I did it would be a hateful
one, and in such sort that I would turn against you at the
judgement-day. God grant that this may not be, but that
you may flower and bring forth fruit, as I said before, and
be all on fire, so that your poor father, who is dying of cold,
may be able to warm himself. No more. — Ever yours, PHILIP
NERI."

That may serve as well as anything else to illustrate
Philip's graceful and playful way of treating women. If so,
the following story illustrates Philip's handling of men.
Francesco Zazzara, a law-student, was one day speaking
of the brilliant plans he had made for his life. Philip seemed
to approve heartily. "Happy you, dear Francesco!" he said;
"you are studying now and one day you will be a doctor of
law and make money and raise your family and perhaps
even become a prelate, till you have nothing more left to
long for. Happy you!" Francesco was delighted and went
on to speak still more fully of his ambitions, till suddenly
Philip drew the young man's head down on his palpitating

---

² Capecelatro says that the "Ragni" was a copyist's mistake and should
have been "Tregui." Ponnelle and Bordet reinstate her as Fiora Ragni.
She does not seem to have been a relative but a young woman who
became one of his penitents soon after his ordination — one would gather
from the letter, the first of his women penitents.

breast and whispered, "*And then?*" There was no need for
him to say anything more. The words came like a revelation to Francesco. He soon afterwards left the world and
entered the Congregation.

Yet in spite of all the immense good he was doing, Philip
was still not quite without enemies, or at any rate without
people who were somewhat critical of his methods. Even
during the somewhat easy-going pontificate of Gregory
XIII — though this spared Philip from much of the espio-
nage and delation to which he had been subjected in the
time of Paul IV and Pius V — he was not entirely free from
troubles. They were, however, slight as compared to the
dangers of the past, and he might at any moment have
ended them, had he chosen to appeal directly to the Pope
who was his friend.

It was during 1579 and 1580 that Attilio Serrano, who was
the vicar of Cardinal Farnese at San Lorenzo in Damaso,
tried to create difficulties. Apparently the Cardinal was annoyed that Philip, whose New Church was technically under
the jurisdiction of the Cardinal of San Lorenzo, had become
virtually independent. By way of asserting his authority, he
prompted Serrano to make enquiries, with the result that
Savelli, the Cardinal-vicar, subjected all of Philip's confessors and preachers to a searching examination. From this
they emerged satisfactorily and Savelli signalised his confidence by appointing Oratorians to hear the confessions of
those imprisoned by the Inquisition.

The claims of jurisdiction, however, were not foregone at
that time, though Philip went so far as to get Anna Borromeo to use her influence with Cardinal Farnese on his behalf. Not until the reign of Sixtus V was the dispute settled.
Then the new pope, coming to hear of the matter, set the
Vallicella completely free of all supervision from San

Lorenzo. It was all the more of a triumph because Sixtus V was one of the most rigorous men ever to occupy the throne of St. Peter. But by then of course not only had Philip's work securely established itself but he was universally regarded as a saint.

Chapter Eleven

ECSTATIC HUMORIST

THE election of Sixtus V took place only because of a fortunate set of accidents. The Emperor did not have time to make his wishes known, and King Philip II, whose influence over the conclave might have proved decisive, also instructed his agents too late. This was providential for the Church, because Spain was now so strong in Europe that, had a Spanish adherent become Pope, the Holy See might have shown itself almost as subservient to the Spanish Crown as it had been to that of France during its Babylonian captivity. Ludwig von Pastor goes so far as to write: "If Philip II had become the absolute master not only of the south of the continent of Europe, but also of the west, how easily he might have transferred the Holy See to Toledo, or have changed Rome itself into a Spanish Avignon." Though Sixtus gave Philip a qualified support against Queen Elizabeth, he admired her brilliancy almost as much as he distrusted the Spanish King's ambition. The story is no doubt apocryphal, but probably gives humorous expression to the Pope's views: according to this he said that it was a pity that he and Elizabeth could not have married, for they would have had children who would have mastered the world. His pontificate was a long struggle against the caesaro-papal pretensions of the King of Spain.

This situation was not at all to Philip Neri's disadvantage. For though his one piece of political activity — his intervention in favor of Henry IV of France — was not to occur for some years, his views about Spanish encroachments were known and coincided with the Pope's opinions. Like Sixtus, Philip wished to see a strong France as a counterweight against the power of Spain. That, like his friendship with the Capuchins, did him no harm with a Pontiff who was still so much of a Franciscan as now and then to put on the Franciscan habit in his private apartments.

Moreover, Sixtus had many other things to think about besides the petty details that had so often been the preoccupation of minds less large and luminous than his own. While anything but neglectful of the reform of the Church, he perceived that his main efforts would have to be directed to securing its independence against secular rulers — which at the moment meant securing its independence against the Most Catholic King. His energies nearer home were directed towards enriching the city of Rome with many magnificent buildings and to suppressing the banditry that had grown to be such a scandal in the papal states. This he put down with such ruthlessness as almost to shock his contemporaries. Whatever severity he had — and he had plenty — was safely drawn off in these channels, so that little was left for the niggling complaints of the jealous and suspicious. During the five years that this really great Pope reigned, Philip Neri was left free to consolidate his work in peace. Though Sixtus had his faults, they, like his distinctive virtues and the virtuosity of his talents, were not of the kind that interfered with such activities as those of the Oratory.

Yet Sixtus thought of himself as one whose destiny it was to complete the work of Pius V. He nearly took the name of his Dominican predecessor, but while in the end deciding upon that of the last Franciscan who had been pope, he at least had the numeral after his name as a connecting link with the great Pius. As Cardinal Montalto he had been given to making savagely caustic remarks about Gregory's mildness. There can be no question about his immense ability and energy. And just then the Church needed on the papal throne a statesman with his vision and courage.

But while directing himself largely to resisting King Philip's caesaro-papism, he interested himself also in the reform of the clergy and the building up of the religious orders. It was at the beginning of his reign in 1585 that St. Camillus de Lellis, who had been one of Philip's penitents, founded his congregation for work in the hospitals, the congregation popularly known as the Fathers of a Good Death. The following year Sixtus canonized another friend of Philip, Felice da Cantalice. It was an event which naturally delighted Philip, as did the conferring of the title of Doctor of the Church upon the Franciscan Bonaventure, and the canonization of the great Dominican missionary, Louis Bertrand.

Philip does not seem to have had much contact with the Jesuits at this time, or since his early friendship with Ignatius and Francis Xavier. He had served with Acquaviva, the Jesuit General, on a commission while Gregory XIII was Pope, but we do not hear of any further relations between the two men. Perhaps the very fact that the Society was passing through a stormy period served to distract attention from Philip's own work and therefore allowed him to pursue it unmolested.

By now he had become a privileged character. His eccentricities were well-known and, so far from exciting criticism, increased the veneration everybody had for him. The Oratory had long ceased to be regarded as a dangerous innovation, and was being frequented largely by the courtiers. Its practice of permitting laymen to discourse during the afternoon sessions had been abandoned, removing what had been a cause of scandal to many. And Sixtus elevated to the cardinalate Federigo Borromeo, the cousin of the dead Charles, and Agostino Cusano, both of whom were devoted to Philip and the Oratory. All these circumstances were very much to Philip's advantage.

The humorous behavior that was so characteristic of him by no means began at this time; it had always been part of his make-up. It does, however, seem to have increased with his sanctity or at any rate to have more freely manifested itself as he grew older. It might almost appear as though he was now able to take advantage of his assured position to indulge his natural propensities, were it not the truer explanation that, the more esteem he was accorded, the more he sought to lessen it by repeating his practice of making himself ridiculous. At the same time there can be no doubt that he enjoyed his own antics and those which he ordered his disciples to perform. If these were a means of mortification, he also relished mischief for its own sweet sake. The chief draw-back now was that as these things had come to be recognised as evidences of spirituality, there arose the danger, as Bacci points out, that they might become occasions of vainglory to those who performed them.

But while Philip was obliged to become more subtle and ingenious in his handling of such devices, he by no means decreased their use. Many of the most famous stories of his whimsicality belong to the later part of his life. Thus there is the incident of the four Polish nobles who called upon him and had to wait while he had some pages of his favorite Mainardi read to him. Every now and then he would stop laughing at the *Facezie* to remark to the Poles,

"You see what capital books I keep and what important matters I have read to me!" They were, of course, utterly mystified and went away with a low opinion of this supposititious saint, which was just what he had intended. Yet his delight in the Florentine humorist was not in the least affected, and we may be sure that he got a good deal of fun out of the situation.

So, too, with another caller, Lorenzo Altieri, who had expected something very different from a humorous Philip. "Why," he said when he left, "he is gay and easy-going, and jokes like anyone else!" When the Fathers of the Oratory begged him to comport himself with more dignity if Altieri should call again, he at once put on a comically sanctimonious look and said, "I suppose that's how you want me to pose!" Then giving his adviser one of those playful blows of his, he said, "Do you not see, animal, that they will say, 'Ah, this Messer Filippo is a saint!' Well, I warn you that if that man comes back I will behave even worse." And he would have done so, too.

It is almost incredible what lengths Philip went to in order to prevent people having a good opinion of him. He would meet the most exalted personages in fantastic dress, or with his clothes worn inside out, or with large white shoes on his feet. At other times he would strut through the streets in the cloak of marten skins given him by Cardinal Gesualdo to make people think that he was vain of his attire; or he would carry a huge bunch of broom in his hand and stop every now and then, pretending to enjoy the delicious scent. On one occasion he had his beard cut on only one side and went out that way, and tried to draw further attention to himself by dancing. On feast days he was quite likely to show himself in church with a jacket over his cassock and his biretta cocked on one side and with a lay-brother who had been told to keep brushing him off. A large blue cushion was sometimes carried on his head in public. Anything to make people think he was foolish!

Nor did his disciples escape having to make themselves ridiculous in the same way. They might be ordered to wear clothes of such a singularity that all passers-by laughed at them. Father Pietro Consolini, whom Philip was very fond of, was a pet victim. He was frequently sent out with purple taffeta and gold lace round his hat. Gallonio had to sing patois songs when there were guests, and the lay-brother Giuliano Macaluffi had to perform rustic dances and once was sent into the refectory during supper carrying on his shoulders a monkey holding a gun and wearing a biretta. It was in vain that the Fathers attempted to hide Macaluffi when this fit was on Philip; he was always dragged out and made to give his exhibition. One young man was sent out with a placard on his back which read, "For eating curds and whey." Another whose piety led him to ask Philip for permission to wear a hair-shirt, got the permission — but also the injunction to wear the hair-shirt outside his coat, a mortification greater than he had bargained for. As "Berto of the hair-shirt" he was jeered at by all Rome. Still another was sent to have his hair trimmed by the Capuchin lay-brother Felice da Cantalice, not knowing that Philip had given private instructions that the whole of his head was to be shaved.

All this added to the gaiety of the city while it developed the humility of Philip's disciples. When Pietro Consolini was preparing a sermon which he had to deliver that afternoon, Philip ordered him to make instead a *lunario*, a comic almanac. And when Agostino Manni, who was in charge of the sermons, found what the preacher was doing and protested to Philip, he was sharply reprimanded. "What do you mean by preaching?" Philip asked in assumed indignation. "What preaching? I am surprised that you should dare to disturb young Consolini. He is doing something of much greater importance than this sermon you are talking about." Poor Manni had to preach the sermon himself. As for the comic almanac, the cardinals to whom it was shown that evening were so amused that they took it away with them to show the Pope, who also may be supposed to have been entertained.

Philip even carried his clowning into church. This was his way of offsetting the many reports that were current that he was favored by God with visions and ecstasies; indeed, it was sometimes to prevent himself from going into an ecstasy that he behaved as he did. On one occasion at least he had his hair cut in church while Mass was being sung, and he took care that people should see what was happening by asking those near by if they did not think he was getting a good barbering. And at the very time when he was being subjected to serious criticism from Attilio Serrano for his alleged ignorance, he deliberately mispronounced some of the Latin words at Mass to encourage this idea when Serrano was present, and afterwards eagerly asked the sacristan whether he had heard any comments. Nobody else would have been so imprudent as that, but of this sort of prudence Philip did not have a particle. It shocked even St. Charles Borromeo, who wrote to his agent in Rome, "You should warn Messer Filippo of the harm he may do by what he says."

The advice was no doubt excellent — for other men. But Philip knew what he was about. Though in the end people came to venerate him all the more because he tried his utmost to destroy their respect, even those who were startled

— like the visiting Poles and Lorenzo Altieri — had no harm done them by Philip's fantasticality. And anyone can see the point of his treatment of Agostino Manni when at the beginning of his career he preached a very eloquent sermon and was therefore ordered to preach it word for word six times running. Philip was afraid that the preacher might get vain. There was no danger of that happening when people groaned to one another every time they saw Manni going into the pulpit, "Here comes the Father who has only one sermon!" His more usual way of control was that of stopping the sermon the moment he thought the preacher got too abstruse or elaborate or showily oratorical.

It is easy to understand how Philip's room, crowded with hilarious young men — among whom none was so gay as the old man with the beautiful white beard and the child's bright blue eyes — was called the School of Christian Mirth. The kind of mortification Philip practiced, and expected them to practice, became almost a kind of game. Those who had been entertained by the whimsical penances laid by Philip on others cheerfully carried out similar penances when their own turn came. The humiliation was imposed on light hearts.

Nor does Philip's humor cease to have its appeal. The one saint about whom the young Goethe got really enthusiastic when writing his *Travels in Italy* is the one he calls the humorous saint. Though it is true that Goethe made a few factual errors and at least one serious error in judgment, his admiration and affection for Philip are evident in all the pages he devotes to him, and he reverts to him several times. "Should one be disposed, as one may well be," he writes, "to question the reality of his reported wonderful power of rising above the ground, there can be no doubt as to his spiritual elevation above this world." But nothing is more attractive to Goethe than Philip's "rich humor." It is still attractive. He would not have been Philip without it.

Without attempting any formal definition of that rather mysterious quality called humor, it might be suggested that it is, at least in part, a special kind of sense of proportion which is delighted rather than distressed by the disproportionateness in things. It is, in other words, a form of judgment. G. K. Chesterton perceived in St. Thomas Aquinas that instantaneous presence of mind which alone deserves the name of wit. And that sort of wit — as distinguished from a mere talent for making smart retorts — cannot be valued enough. All the same humor is something still higher. It is also more practical, for it is a species of common sense. This common sense underlay all of Philip's so-called eccentricity. He did not enjoy his humor any the less because he put it to a useful purpose, and no doubt he often made jokes and did laughable things without any special object in mind. But it is evident that just as often he had an object quite practical. It was with jests that he drew men to God.

It was with jests, too, that he developed his own spiritual life. His gaiety was an important element in his spirituality, and it was employed for a definite purpose. So intense was his sense of God that he was always afraid it would so overwhelm him as to make him unable to get through his external religious duties. He also was afraid that at any moment he would be rapt into an ecstasy while he was in the company of others. For this reason when he went into a church he usually dared not stay longer than was necessary for the saying of an Our Father and a Hail Mary. For this reason when in 1590 he was presented with the bodies of the martyrs St. Papias and St. Maurus for his New Church, he had to resist the danger of being overcome by going up to a

Swiss Guard who had a magnificent beard and stroking it. He was not in the least restrained by the presence of ten cardinals. For this reason he was obliged — as on the Wednesday of Holy Week in 1579 — to play with the keys of his room and a sun-dial during the reading of the Passion. And for this reason, too, he had to collect himself before saying Mass by first reading a page or two of Mainardi's *Facezie*. Laughter, in his case, went with holiness; his laughter further served the purpose of preventing people from discovering how holy he was.

In this he did not always succeed. If he did not give himself away, his intimates were likely to do so. Thus when he was at the house of the Marchesa Rangoni the Countess Olivares, the wife of the Spanish Ambassador, asked him how long it was since he had forsaken the world. Philip answered lightly, "I don't know that I have ever left it." In proof of this he turned to Gallonio, who was there with him, and asked, "Antonio, don't I still take pleasure in pretty books and stories and poetry?" To which Gallonio gave the answer, "Yes, but that's the only way you can moderate the ardor of your love of God." On the way home Philip disgustedly said to his too candid young friend, "That was a fine answer you gave, Antonio; may God forgive you!"

It was not to be expected, of course, that ecstasy and humor show themselves in him simultaneously, but sometimes humor and fervor did. Thus when Philip was being pressed by Gregory XIV and then Clement VIII to accept the cardinalate, if anybody referred to this, he had a way of taking off his biretta and tossing it in the air, crying, "Paradiso, Paradiso!" — from which they were at liberty to make anything they chose. As the Abbé Ponnelle remarks, "He seems to have had two characteristic sides, ecstatic fervor on the one hand and picturesque expansiveness on the other." They balanced and completed one another in him.

Like all the greater mystics, he attached little value to ecstasies as such. In this he resembled St. Teresa of Àvila, who was born the same year as himself and who was to be canonized with him. He tried to resist ecstasies and, when unable to do so, still had no complacency in them. He would have thoroughly concurred in St. Teresa's saying that if she, in preference to others, was led by this extraordinary way, it was due to her weakness, which needed such special support. One day, only a few years before his death, when Bordini had been preaching about ecstasies, Philip did what he rarely did at that time and went into the pulpit immediately after him. But instead of being able to speak, he was seen to be trembling violently and weeping. By degrees he managed to pull himself together — by tugging at his beard and passing his hands over his face. Then a few broken words came from him: "He who wishes for ecstasies is greatly deceiving himself, for he does not know what an ecstasy is."[1] He could say no more. From the pulpit he went straight to the sacristy.

Perhaps because he was so deeply impressed by that scene, Bordini wrote of Philip: "It is an amazing thing how he, who was favored with so many colloquies with God, who so constantly experienced the divine sweetness, who was endowed by heaven with such extraordinary gifts, looked upon it as fallacious and perilous in the extreme for spiritual men to seek after visions and revelations; he sharply rebuked those who took pleasure in such things, and de-

---

[1] The best authorities make a distinction between the mystical state and what, when they occur, are to be described as only the concomitant phenomena of ecstasy. It is these phenomena that Philip was referring to, knowing as he did, that they can be pathological, or diabolical, or fraudulent and not easily distinguished from those of genuine mystical ecstasy.

clared that there was no snare of the devil into which it was easier for men to fall than into follies such as these." Bacci further explains that Philip considered it difficult to have a vision without being puffed up by the fact, still more difficult to think oneself unworthy, and most difficult of all to prefer patience, obedience, and humility to the sweetness experienced by the ecstatic. Ponnelle makes the subtler psychological suggestion that Philip may well have feared that if he gave himself up to these celestial favors they might have degenerated into something quite different. However that may be, it is certain that Philip was always highly distrustful of such things. He would not allow that there was even much value in the gift of tears, which he himself had to an extraordinary degree. "Why, the very prostitutes," he used to say, "will weep if one talks to them of God!" Once found by a great dignitary weeping over what he was reading, Philip passed it all off with a joke. "Why shouldn't a poor orphan like me cry?" he asked.

It was the same with putting any faith in dreams or prophecies. At a decisive moment in his life he had had a vision, or perhaps a dream, of St. John the Baptist. And — apart from the visions we may suppose him to have concealed — we know he had a vision of Christ and another of our Lady. But although he never denied their reality, he continued to think that such manifestations might be fallacious and were to be guarded against rather than sought. "It is a dangerous thing to put credence in dreams," he used to say. "It is by being a good man and a good Christian that one gets to Paradise."

As for the predictions about which we hear so much in his biographers, while there is no reason to doubt that they were made, it is easy to see how many of the predictions instanced may have been no more than shrewd inferences —

the kind of predictions we all make without becoming or claiming to be true prophets. But there are cases not so readily to be explained on those grounds. It was Philip himself who confided to Cardinal Federigo Borromeo: "It sometimes happens to me that I say things without knowing why I say them; it is God who makes me speak." Here as elsewhere in Philip, however, the natural and the supernatural were so closely related that it is not always possible to distinguish clearly between them.

Philip had no illusions in regard to revelations and the like in their relation to sanctity. It is a mere matter of history that many of the greatest of saints never had such experiences at all, and that those to whom they have come have virtually unanimously declared that they should not be relied on too much. Though the world is disposed to measure the mystics by the yardstick of the marvels related of them, that is not the measure of the mystics themselves. And of no mystic is this more true than of Philip Neri.

His conviction that the majority of visions are delusions — either of the devil or one's own imagination — explains his treatment of the celebrated ecstatic, Orsola Benincasa, during the seven months she spent in Rome in 1582. Gregory appointed Philip to serve on a commission to enquire into her case. Though the other members included two cardinals and Monsignor Speciano and Tarugi and the General of the Jesuits, Acquaviva, it was Philip who seems to have conducted most of the actual investigation.

Even now it is easy enough to understand his strong prejudice against Orsola when we read the glibness of the words in which she spoke of her ecstasies; it was all so different from his own habit of reserve. At the same time he does seem to have been unduly hard on her, for he said many harsh and even threatening things to her in his efforts to force an admission of fraud or of diabolical possession. Capecelatro does his best to soften Philip's behavior, but even Philip's final judgement was not as favorable as Capecelatro would have us believe. It was merely that Orsola had shown herself humble and submissive under his tests and that he therefore could not maintain that his suspicions of her were proved. Five years later Germanico Fedeli wrote as his secretary to Tarugi: "As to Father [Giovenale] Ancina, our Father Messer Filippo is much grieved; he is afraid that this has come through Orsola, whose spirit is so dangerous to herself and others, for one can see nothing in her which leads one to believe that she is led by the Spirit of God. Yet the Father, who has always shrunk from this sort of thing as being extremely dangerous, does not wish to injure this woman any more than those who, led perhaps by an excess of simplicity, put their faith in her, and even go so far as to follow her along this way of visions, revelations and personal sentiments." One is touched by Orsola's complete lack of animosity towards one whom she might have been pardoned for looking upon as her enemy. Several times it was through her influence that benefits were conferred on the Oratory. Her charity is really very impressive. Yet Philip never completely changed his judgement about her; that she claimed to have visions and revelations was, to Philip's mind, a very bad sign.

Yet times without number we are told of people who saw Philip in ecstasy and even in the state of what is called levitation. The evidence is so explicit and comes from so many quarters that it cannot be disregarded, except by one who is prepared to make the dogmatic affirmation that such phenomena are impossible. While there may be a natural explanation which would cover some of these cases, with the still greater possibility that there are natural manifestations

which are a kind of counterpart to those that are really
supernatural, the fact itself must be admitted by an open
mind. Along with that fact goes the other that Philip did
not wish such things to happen to him, that he did his best
to prevent them from happening, and that when they did
happen he tried to conceal them. It is, of course, likely that
many of his ecstasies were hardly more than prolonged fits
of abstraction. He usually got somebody to say office with
him in case he should become so lost in contemplation that
he could not finish it by himself. At a word about God, or
before a picture of the Blessed Virgin, his eyes would fill
with tears and he might be drawn out of himself. And here,
in the warning he gives to others, he may offer some explanation of his own case: he always told his penitents not
to fix their eyes too intently on pictures or images, or to
gaze at them too long, as doing so might open the way to
illusions — that is, that they might induce autohypnosis. But
after all subtractions have been made, there is no doubt
that Philip was one of the greatest ecstatics who ever lived.

The most important fact of all is his extraordinary way of
saying Mass at the end of his life. Gregory gave him permission in January, 1591, to say it in private in a room close
to his own. Then the server used to leave him at the *Agnus
Dei,* after having extinguished the candles, drawn the shutters, and lit a small lamp in the darkened room. On the door
he hung a sign reading, "Silence — the Father is saying
Mass." Two hours later he would return and if, upon knock-
ing, he got any response, he would go in and light the
candles again and open the shutters. This would bring
Philip back, and the rest of the Mass would be said. Until
this permission was given, Philip had always had to hurry
through the Holy Sacrifice for fear that he might be seized
by an ecstasy or fall into abstraction and so be unable to

go any further. In his old age he was able to indulge himself; yet he continued to advise the Fathers of the Congregation to say Mass as rapidly as was consistent with seemliness; their rooms, in his frequently expressed opinion, and not the altar, were the only place where it was permissible for them to surrender themselves to their private devotion.

What happened in that little darkened chapel nobody knows. If there were any visions or ecstasies Philip never told anybody, unless it was his confessor. All that we can be sure is that it was intense prolonged prayer, the prayer of the mystic united to God. As to its nature we have no right to speculate, and any speculations would be in vain. Like his server, we must leave him there alone with his Lord.

Those who saw him when he emerged saw a face so wasted that it seemed that he was on the point of expiring. Exhausted from his experience, Philip would throw himself on his bed. Whenever this was possible, he tried to be alone for two or three hours afterwards. That was not often. For visitors were always liable to call and were always received when they did. To meet them was leaving Christ for Christ.

Chapter Twelve

APOSTLE OF ROME

IT MAY have been that when passing through Rome, on his way to San Germano in 1533, Philip had an intimation that his life-work was to be there. Certainly his was a work that was almost exclusively for Rome, the city he never left for over sixty years. In one sense his apostolate may be said to have begun from the moment of his arrival, and to have been exercised even during those eighteen years he lived there as a hermit, dividing his time between the catacomb of San Sebastiano and his pilgrimages to the Seven Churches and his little room in the house of Galeotto del Caccia. It was, however, only by degrees that the special nature of his apostolate was made plain. It was only in his later years that he was recognised to be the Apostle of Rome.

There were many other great men — saints and reformers — whose work was done in that city. St. Ignatius, for example, set up there the center for directing his operations. But just because his plan of campaign embraced the world his activities at Rome were of an incidental and subsidiary character, important as these were. Of all those who lived their lives there not one had anything comparable to the effect Philip exercised upon the lives of the Roman people. He was at once a character known to everybody, their oracle and their saint. As Pastor remarks: "His apostolate extended down from the Pope to the smallest urchin in the streets."

It must be remembered that though his main work was done at the Oratory, he never waited there for people to go to him. Though it was no longer necessary for him to hunt down his quarry in the Banchi, the moment the exercises were over, he would go out for a walk accompanied by a gay group of his disciples. But these little excursions, which were so familiar a sight, were not merely for recreation. Philip still went twice a week to visit the prisons and even more often would drop in at one of the hospitals. When he was unable to go himself, he would send his young men on missions of charity.

By means of them he contrived to conceal his own charity. If he wished to keep himself out of sight — usually in order to spare the recipients of his alms from knowing whence they came — one of his disciples would be commissioned to carry food or clothing or money to those in need. But there were many occasions when the most confidential way of managing affairs was to go in secret himself. Cardinal Bellarmine (who was himself to be canonized) said when he was in charge of Philip's Process that here was one who deserved to be called a second St. John the Almoner. And a poor woman exclaimed in 1608, on hearing of the canonization of Francesca Romana, "And when are they going to canonize my Father Philip? Countless times he has come to my house with bread under his cloak and money in his pockets!"

Philip's charities were not merely wide-spread; they were very lavish. When Animuccia died, for example, Philip made himself responsible for his daughters and looked after them until they became nuns, at which time he provided them with suitable dowries. And if in that case he may be considered to have had a kind of obligation, because of the services that Animuccia had rendered to the Oratory, there

were many other cases in which the only claim upon him
was one of need. For four years Philip looked after a widow
and her four children, along with their grandmother. And
these were only two instances out of many that might be
cited.

People often surmised that he must be miraculously supplied with money, so much of it did he distribute. And that
may be so. However, Philip had his own way of getting hold
of what he needed, as when he came to the rescue of two
old Frenchmen who were watchmakers and were finding it
difficult to dispose of their wares. To help them he kept a
large number of their watches in his own room and sold
them himself, sometimes several to one person. Perhaps this
may be considered as taking a slightly unfair advantage of
his visitors, and there were those who were rather scandalised at Philip's persuading people to throw away their
money in what they considered to be foolish ways. But
Philip had no scruples on the point. The watchmakers were
in straits; that was enough for him. As Bacci remarks, "There
were no bounds to his tenderness towards the bashful poor."

But, of course, it was not his charities that kept Philip in
Rome; he would have found ample opportunities for them
anywhere. It was the spiritual work he was doing among
the Romans that held him tethered fast. There had been
moments during the pontificate of Pius V when he had been
almost tempted to yield to the pressure of St. Charles Borromeo and transfer the Oratory to Milan. Yet in spite of the
opposition — and even the obloquy — he encountered at that
time, he hung on, believing in some change of fortune, or
rather convinced in the depths of his being that God intended him to remain in Rome. Though later he did allow
the establishment of what might be described as a Milan
branch, it was only for a short time. And one cannot but

feel that Philip was almost glad to have a clash of opinion
between St. Charles and himself as a pretext for recalling
his disciples. Negotiation could have removed the misunderstanding. Philip's real objection to Milan was that it diverted
part of his energies. He wished everything to be concentrated in Rome.

Yet in spite of himself he came to be saddled with some
outside responsibilities. One of these occurred when the
Abbate Navarro ceded to Philip his commendatory abbey in
the Abruzzi. It was accepted reluctantly, though it carried
with it the reversion of the revenues when Navarro should
die. Even so, Philip probably would not have accepted the
gift had he realised all that it would entail. For though the
abbey itself was extinct, the abbot had such wide spiritual
jurisdiction as to be virtually a bishop, and he also had
temporal authority in the district. Of these powers Philip
made Talpa the administrator. But eventually the charge
was surrendered gladly to the Archbishop of Chieti.

But at least no Oratory was established there. As for the
Oratory at San Severino, where three priests were permitted
to affiliate themselves with Philip's Congregation, it was on
the strict understanding that Philip should supply no men
and should never be called upon to do so. The connection
was therefore nominal. It was a cardinal point with him not
to do anything that might drain away his resources from
Rome.

There was, however, the great foundation of Naples, about
which a few words should be said. That it was made at
all represents a partial departure from Philip's original plans,
just as some of the customs of the community there showed
for a time a tendency to a greater degree of monasticism,
properly so called, than met with Philip's approval. In this
matter, as the Abbé Bordet says, his hand was forced.

It happened in this way. The brilliant and somewhat rest-less Tarugi had always advocated an extension of work and had with some difficulty been resisted by Philip. It was Tarugi that Charles Borromeo specially sought for Milan, and Tarugi had wanted to go, in the hope of initiating the wider activities of which he dreamed. When the Milan project finally fell through, Tarugi, who was a sufferer from sciatica, went to Ischia for the baths, and while at Naples he preached with such success that he was begged to re-main and establish an Oratory. Nobody was more willing to do so than himself, but nobody could have been much less willing than Philip. It was in vain that the Archbishop — who had asked for an Oratory as early as 1577 — himself came up from Naples to Rome, promising almost anything to get Tarugi and a group of the Fathers. Philip still would not consent to a permanent foundation. Tarugi was indeed allowed to go again to his sulphur baths, and again he preached at Naples. But not until 1586 did Philip agree to the formal establishment of the Naples house. That he did so at all was mainly because he could not help himself; a group of his subjects had worked behind his back and he found himself committed to something of which at heart he disapproved.

If he took up the attitude he did, this was not solely because he feared that Naples would drain his resources at Rome, though that was the reason he always gave. Another reason, hardly less strong, was his fear that this would prove to be the first move towards turning the Congregation into a religious order. He was well aware that some of the Fathers hoped for this, or at any rate believed such a de-velopment to be inevitable. His idea of the Congregation — the idea that eventually prevailed — was that it should re-main a group of secular priests, bound in no way except by voluntary charity. Therefore, while blessing Tarugi and his companions on their departure, Philip told them, "You want to go, but I am not of the opinion that you should go." And when, shortly before he died, he was begged to express his approval of the Naples foundation, he would answer no more than, "If it does not please me, how can I say so?"

Coincident with the establishment of the Naples Oratory, and not unconnected with that event, was Philip's acceptance in 1587 of the office of Provost for life. It was a position which, according to the rules, was intended to last only for three years; but Philip gave way under the arguments of those who said that, in his case, an exception had to be made. His modesty was overcome by the necessity he felt of keeping the whole group of Oratorians under his jurisdiction. Not yet had the principle of complete autonomy for each house of the Congregation been ratified.

Yet Philip was extremely disinclined to appear as any sort of superior. That was why he had never lived at San Giovanni, though for thirteen years he had been its rector. Nor for the same reason would he go to live at the Vallicella until 1583, but retained the quarters he had occupied at San Girolamo since his ordination in 1551. There from the Church of the Florentines — and, since 1576, from the Vallicella — the Fathers had been obliged to go to Philip's room every morning for confession; back again in the afternoon for the exercises; and finally in the evening for the hour of prayer.

It was obviously an inconvenient arrangement for them, yet Philip had refused to listen when they begged him to live with them. If he had objected to move in 1564, when he accepted the direction of San Giovanni, lest this would make his control evident, he wanted to do so still less after the Congregation had been founded, for then he would have been obliged to appear publicly as its founder, something very disturbing to his humility. He therefore always contrived to evade the issue and to go on living where he was. It is a signal proof of the force of Philip's example and the resplendence of the Philippine spirit that he had been able to exercise his authority without actually residing among his subjects. All the same the situation was too anomalous to last indefinitely.

In this he was humored for a long while. In the end, however, the Fathers at the Vallicella approached Cardinal Cesi, their great benefactor, to see if he could not persuade Philip to join them. The cardinal, instead of attempting persuasion, which might have been of no use, went to the Pope, and Gregory XIII gave Philip a formal obedience to leave San Girolamo at once. It was on November 22, 1583, that this was done. Then accompanied by some of his disciples carrying his belongings — including a kettle and a frying-pan and other kitchen utensils, for whatever cooking he did during these later years was done in his own rooms — he set out for his new abode. On the way there they had to pass the Corte Savella prison, and the jailbirds were vastly entertained by this procession of fine young gentlemen carrying pots and pans. With affable insults they jeered, and when one of them called from behind the bars, "Father, fry us some pancakes!" Philip was delighted. Bacci, of course, gives this as another instance of Philip's love of mortification. And so no doubt it was. Yet one suspects that Philip himself thought the scene very amusing. And by this time his disciples must have been well schooled in all the arts of making themselves ridiculous.

It was characteristic of him, too, that he should have kept the key of his old rooms at San Girolamo. By this means he could bring almost himself to believe that he had not really given them up but was at the Vallicella only on a visit. He not only frequently went back to San Girolamo but he left his cat behind. It served to show that the rooms were still his and also made itself useful for purposes of mortification; one or other of his young men was sent every day to see that the animal was fed.

The great thing, however, was that the Fathers now had Philip safe at the Vallicella. Even so he did his best to conceal the fact that he was the Provost, and would not allow himself to be addressed by any higher title than "Father." He took very little part in the community life, continuing to take his poor meals by himself, and occupying rooms in the most remote part of the house. Again he built a *loggia* where he could retire for prayer. But he now always attended the exercises, and he was immediately accessible to any of the Congregation who wished to consult him.

We have many details of his life at this time. He still used to pray at night with a lamp darkened except on the side which threw a beam on his crucifix. It was noticed that he never knelt when anyone else was present, but sat or stood, lest the kneeling posture itself should be too much for his emotions and bring on an ecstasy. It was also noticed that now he had quite overcome his repugnance to have a chalice or a drinking glass that anybody else used. And so far from displaying his former fastidiousness about his vestments, he would say to the sacristan, "Give me the oldest you have; the good ones are not for me." At night when he went to bed he arranged within reach a figure of our Lord that had been detached from a crucifix, and a rosary. This was so that he could pray the moment he awoke. Bacci records that by merely touching the watch at the head of his bed he could tell what time it was. Something preternatural has been drawn from this fact, but the explanation may be that the

watch had no crystal so that the position of the hands, felt
in the dark, could have let Philip know the hour. His was
at all events a simple, humble, and retired life. Its chief
secrets were not confided even to those closest to him.

Though everything in the Congregation depended upon
Philip — something he did his best not to admit openly but
which everybody knew to be the case — he was loath to
exercise any authority. The Provost, according to the rules
in force, was assisted by four Deputies, the senior of whom
held the position of local rector. Philip rarely attended their
meetings, even after he went to live at the Vallicella. Ordinarily he left them perfectly free. Not he but the Rector
drew up the agenda, and though Philip was sometimes rep-
resented by his secretary, this was mainly in order that he
might get a report as to what had been discussed. He did
not always agree with the decisions but he usually accepted
them.

There were times, however, when apparently quite un-
accountably, he used his power of veto. But this seemed
unaccountable only because Philip did not reach his conclusions by the ordinary process of weighing pros and cons
— such discussions were not to his taste and were apt to
leave him confused; he was guided instead by his own inspirations, and therefore he must on occasion have seemed
to the others rather capricious. Precisely because he could
not always give a reason for his opinion, and also because
he was afraid to trust his inspirations too far, he asserted
himself very rarely — one might say never, unless he was
perfectly sure that his inspirations came from the Holy
Ghost. When he did suddenly put his foot down, then everybody had to submit. His normal method has been described
by Fedeli: "He tells us his wishes, and if there is opposition,
he accepts the views of others."

Many of the Fathers of his Congregation were aware of his inspirations and came to know by experience that his inner guide was more safely to be trusted than their own judgment. Thus on October 26, 1584, Tarugi wrote to Bordini: "Where is that confidence and obedience that formerly we used to show towards our beloved Father? . . . Let us, my very dear brother, bear with this old man as long as he is alive, because we shall weep for him when he is dead, and we shall understand him better than we do now." As that was not explicit enough, he added in a postscript: "I have always had reason to repent when I have gone against the commands of the Father, even sometimes when I had what seemed to me good reasons. . . . We wish to know more about it than we should, and attribute to ourselves the Spirit which God has given to the Father for our direction; his advice has never been at fault. What he has said to us has always been right, and he must be our rule as long as he lives." This we may take to be the general view, but as the Fathers were human, they did on occasion try to get round Philip by cajolery and argument and even by proceeding against his known wishes. It was so in the case of the founding of the house at Naples, and when it prospered in spite of Philip's forebodings, it was Tarugi who made the subacid comment, "The prophets do not prophesy every day."

One gets the impression that Philip was all the more dubious about the project because it was to some extent inspired by Orsola Benincasa. Her confessor was Alessandro Borla, an Oratorian lent to the service of the Archbishop of Naples. And it was her friend the Abbate Navarro whom she had prompted to give the Oratorians the house in which they first lived as well as the abbey which proved to be such a burden to them. Tarugi attributed to the prayers of her community the success of his own preaching. But Philip may well have been all the more hesitant because she was mixed up in the affair. He still could not bring himself to believe in the genuineness of her mystical gifts, and in fact she was not always a good prophet, as when she foretold that the Abbate Navarro would be the "Papa Angelicus" of that fascinating but spurious document which passes as the prophecies of St. Malachy.

The fact that Sister Orsola, so far from bearing any resentment against Philip, did her utmost to further the work of the Oratory at Naples must be taken to prove that she was a good Christian although she was not a genuine visionary. It should, however, be said that even had she not come into the picture at all, Philip would still have been against carrying his work to Naples.

This was not because he was in principle opposed to making foundations outside of Rome. As the Abbé Bordet remarks: "It would be more true to say that he acquiesced in principle . . . [but] his own genius was not directed towards these distant foundations; besides the fact that his humility shrank from the prominence which the multiplications of Oratories would give to his own office of Provost, he had no real interest except in what he could see and touch, in what fell under his direct perception, in what immediately concerned him." Thus to the Bishop of Fermo, who had asked for an establishment there, he had replied in 1580: "The Lord knows that it is not only my desire, but that of all the Congregation, that this our institute of the Oratory should spread far and wide; and we should gladly devote ourselves to this work were it clear to us that this was our proper vocation." He falls back upon his usual argument — that he has been obliged to refuse the Bishops of Milan and Bologna for the same reason that he must now refuse the Bishop of Fermo; namely, that he does not have a sufficient number of men for more than was being done in Rome.

Never once did Philip visit the house at Naples, though Giovanale Ancina tried to entice him there with glowing descriptions of the marvellous climate and scenery. Even these allurements could not draw him from Rome. He could always excuse himself on the ground that he was too old to make an arduous journey. And a balmy climate was nothing to a man who, even in the depth of winter, could not bear to wear many clothes but had to go about with his cassock unbuttoned because of the heat of his body, and who often laughed at his younger disciples because they felt the cold so much more than he did. As for scenery, he had a wonderful view over Rome from his *loggia*. With that and with his work at Rome he was content. He kept an anxious eye over Naples but left the Fathers there pretty much to their own devices, though disliking some semi-monastic practices that were being introduced among them. He disapproved, for instance, of their view concerning the individual's ownership of private property, and their adoption of a cassock which had about it a little of the look of a habit, and their use of the title "Father" instead of the "Messer" then customary for secular priests. But he let these matters pass, accepting what he could not prevent except by the exercise of an authority he sought to avoid.

If he consented only reluctantly to the establishment of the Oratory at Naples, he also tried to avoid getting involved in other external activities. Here he was skilful in making evasions, but here, too, he was sometimes overborne. The Congregation — or rather Bordini — went over his head in re-establishing the exercises at San Giovanni in 1584. A rescue work for fallen women initiated by the Marchesa Rangoni received Philip's help. And the Fathers took over the direction of the short-lived Polish college in Rome. It had Philip's sympathy because of the efforts being made by Stephen Bathori and Queen Anne to bring their country back to the Catholic faith. But the work was one that, after all, lay outside the true sphere of the Oratory. Philip's whole idea was to conserve all his forces for the Vallicella and, since Naples had been established, for that house. He did not want to go beyond what he felt to be his proper field.

What he could not do was to prevent the creation all over Italy of Oratories founded in imitation of his own, nor did he wish to prevent this, as these oratories remained un-affiliated. They were, however, thought of as institutes that might eventually become part of his Congregation, which did happen later on in some cases. But Philip had a positive horror of being the "General" of a new order, and so took the consistent line that he did not have enough formed men to spare except for what he had already undertaken.

Against this it might be urged that, had he been willing to branch out, he would not have lacked recruits. If men — especially mature men of parts — were in some instances reluctant to join him, this was because they knew they would be restricted by doing so. This was why many of his more ardent disciples entered one or other of the existing religious orders and why every now and then even some of the Fathers at the Vallicella would depart for a wider sphere of activity. In spite of this, Philip held to his original purpose, even when he did not insist on it. No propulsion ever came from him; rather he was a brake upon the more impetuous of his subjects.

If the question be merely the abstract one as to whether the work should have been extended or restricted, Philip may or may not have been right. Certainly many of his most gifted followers believed that he was not right. But such a discussion is futile, because of leaving out of consideration the make-up of the man who had to do the work. He knew that he was not fitted for any task except the one he was performing. There was another important consideration; the Oratory at Rome was itself somewhat in decline, because Tarugi and Talpa had gone to Naples and the almost equally brilliant Bordini was on the point of getting himself taken into the entourage of Cardinal Aldobrandini, the future Clement VIII, when that dignitary was sent on a diplomatic mission to Poland. With these three men lost, and with Philip now old and infirm, it was inevitable that some of the Oratory's former glory should depart.

It was only Philip's own glory that did not diminish. His sanctity burned more brightly every day and his influence grew greater. That made up for everything else. Though he would have protested violently against the title, he was already being called the Apostle of Rome. It was recognised that nobody had ever done what he was doing there. We should see that he could not have done it had he not concentrated upon a sole object.

There was one instance, and only one instance, of his willingly going beyond that field. This was when he interested himself in the matter of the reconciliation of King Henry IV of France to the Church. This time he not only ventured into politics but took extreme and almost high-handed measures to make his views prevail.

This is a question from which the machinations of Philip II cannot be eliminated. That king came to look upon himself as being more Catholic than the Pope and in certain things even to act within his own dominions as another pope. Pius V had put up with this because of his personal regard for the Spanish monarch and because he believed that Philip II was, after all, the most devoted champion of Catholic interests — a view that was, in general, shared by Gregory XIII. Sixtus V, however, took a very different line and vigorously opposed Philip's caesaro-papism. The result was that at the conclave held after the death of Sixtus, Spanish influence was brought to bear to see to it that a Pope acceptable to Spain was elected. At once the question of the right of the King of Navarre came up, and Bonelli, the cardinal-nephew, actually maintained in the conclave that the French cardinals who had adhered to Navarre had by that fact become schismatics and so should not be admitted. The move was impolitic and failed. And the fact that Spain listed no less than thirty cardinals as *personae non gratae* brought about a revulsion of feeling, with the result that Clement VII was elected.

But Clement lived for only thirteen days, during most of which he was ill. At the second conclave held in 1590, Cardinal Sfondrato was chosen and took the name of Gregory XIV. He was a man who regarded King Philip as one upon whom the Catholic cause depended. With his election Spain had triumphed after all.

But Spain's triumph was brief. Gregory XIV lasted for just over ten months. And the new Pope, Clement VIII, had as one of his most pressing problems the question of Henry and the French throne, a question which depended upon the genuineness of Henry's reconciliation with the Church.

It was a question not so simple as it seemed. For it was complicated by the Spanish policy which sought to weaken France, something that could be best done by supporting the League against Henry. In Rome every effort was made by the Spanish partisans to cast doubts on the sincerity of Henry's conversion. Spain did not want to see France united behind her king.

Another political consideration entered in. Though it is

perfectly true that the Most Christian Kings frequently showed themselves willing to act in much the same way as the Most Catholic King, and though the old axiom *Gesta Dei per Francos* tended to become in practice that the deeds of the French were the deeds of God,[1] the immediate necessity was that of preventing Philip from becoming a kind of arch-pope, and the immediate means of doing so was that of uniting a strong France under Henry of Navarre.

On the other hand, it could not be denied that Spain and the League had good reasons, or what appeared to be such, for being suspicious of Henry. He had become a Catholic twice before, and each time had reverted to Protestantism for his political advantage. How could anyone — so it was argued — trust such a man? As he was a relapsed heretic his case had to be referred to the Holy See for final decision. And Clement, never given to acting very promptly, was put in a very difficult position.

Henry used several special emissaries and ambassadors, Cardinals Gondi and Ossat, as well as Brulard de Sillery, and wrote in his own hand to the Pope in 1592. And at the end of 1593 the Duc de Nevers arrived at Rome on the same business.

Nevers was an adroit — almost too adroit — ambassador. But he also could be tactless, as when this descendent of the Imperial Paleogus — he was also of the Gonzaga family — wrote to the Queen Mother in France (a Medici): "The Gonzagas were princes long before the Medici were gentlemen." And Sillery was equally tactless in trying to press handsome gifts upon Baronius, who, as confessor to the Pope, was in a position to further Henry's

---

[1] The sincerity of this conviction is, of course, the best that can be said for the power politics of Richelieu and that strange Capuchin mystic Père Joseph.

cause. But Nevers did the best thing possible in going to
see Philip Neri to enlist his support. Philip, who received
the duke in bed, had one of his special illuminations on
that occasion.

The situation was very dangerous. The French Church, or
an important section of it, had ignored the Pope in absolv-
ing Henry and in giving him coronation and unction in
Chartres Cathedral on February 27, 1594. A French schism
and the appointment of a French Patriarch threatened if
Henry was rejected by the Holy See, and some of the Spanish representatives at Rome hinted that Spain would be
split from the Roman obedience should the Pope accept
Henry as a child of the Church. As whatever Clement did
was likely to be wrong, he delayed about reaching any decision. It was at this point that Philip Neri took a hand in
the affair.

It would be altogether too much to say that his was the
deciding influence, for though Clement had been a penitent
of his for thirty years before ascending the papal throne,
and though he had enormous veneration for Philip, on matters of this sort he reached his own conclusions. But Philip
at least had a good deal to do with the outcome; for the
first and last time in his life he exercised pressure in a political matter and did not hesitate to say that he was inspired
by the Holy Ghost. Cardinals Cusano and Federigo Borromeo — both Spanish adherents — did shake him for a moment, but only for a moment. Baronius and Tomaso Bozio,
the historians, supported his intuitions with their own array
of historical facts, and he became as firm as ever in support
of Henry.

He now took an extraordinary step by letting the Pope
know that he would withdraw Baronius from his office as
Clement's confessor unless judgment in Henry's favor was

delivered. It seemed to him essential that France should be strengthened as a counterweight to Spain — not merely for political reasons but for the good of the Church as a whole. In the end, as we know, King Henry IV was reconciled by the Holy See and remained at least ostensibly a Catholic to the day of his death. There can be no doubt that the result was very much for the benefit of Christendom. Ludwig von Pastor credits the Jesuit Cardinal Toledo and Baronius and Philip as the chief instruments for bringing about this termination of the case.

Baronius had already dedicated the third volume of his *Annals* to Philip II. It was done at the suggestion of Philip, who hoped that it would be accepted as a kind of peace offering, making amends for what Baronius had said about Spain and Sicily. The king, however, showed his cold resentment by never sending a word of acknowledgement. Henry IV also had a long memory and was duly grateful for what had been done for him. When he received the dedication of the ninth volume of the *Annals,* he wrote Baronius a letter of thanks in which he addressed him as *Mon Cousin.* By that time Philip, to whom the French king owed even more, was dead.

Chapter Thirteen

SAINT IN ALABASTER

WRITING to his brother in 1575, Giovenale Ancina, who was then a young doctor, described Philip as he was at sixty: "He is a beautiful old man, clean and white, like an ermine; his flesh is delicate and virginal, and if, when he lifts his hand, he holds it up to the sun, it is transparent like alabaster." If Philip was like that then, he must have been still more ethereal when he was eighty. Even if we ascribe to their enthusiastic imagination the odor of sanctity people said his aged body gave out, it is certainly true that the slight little man grew slighter and even daintier the nearer he drew to the grave. Always he had been excessively fastidious, with St. Bernard's saying often on his lips — "Poverty I love, but not dirt." But now he had gone back — because he felt that he had at last conquered his repugnance to using anything touched by other lips — to a cup (one of coarse glass) used only by himself and to a private chalice. Never had he been anything but very particular about his clothes; shabby as they were, and often fantastic, they were always spotless. Odd as he might look, his was a distinction that suggested something not of this earth.

He had never been accustomed to eat much. But now, after having slightly mitigated for a time his early diet of a daily roll and a few olives, he reverted to something almost as severe. When he had visitors or was with the community in the refectory, he took pains to conceal his abstemiousness and pretended to eat what others ate so as not to appear singular. But in his own room, where he usually took his meals, he never allowed himself meat, or even fish or cheese or milk. His first meal, taken about two in the afternoon — for he said Mass very late, and with him it lasted two hours — consisted of a morsel of bread dipped in wine. "I could have swallowed all that served him as a meal in a single mouthful," declared one of the witnesses at his Process. His dinner at this period consisted of a roll and an egg and a tiny flask of wine. That he might have the satisfaction of living entirely on alms, he accepted these provisions from others — Cardinals Federigo Borromeo and Cusano and Montalto claiming the privilege of supplying them. Even from this little supply he found that he could give something away, and at dinner he now rarely put any wine into the water he drank. Sometimes it was noticed that the food in his room remained untouched. When his attention was drawn to it, he would answer, "Ah yes, I must have forgotten all about it!" He jested about his scarecrow thinness by saying that he did not eat because he had no wish to become as fat as Francesco Scarlatti, a merchant famous for his corpulence.

His abstemiousness was not due solely to austerity. He was accustomed to warn his disciples against undermining their constitutions in this way, as such damage once done could not easily be repaired. In Philip's case there was an increasing repugnance to food. He said that it was only by a spare diet that he was able to cool the excessive heat of his body. But it worried those around him to see him so "dried up, thin, and emaciated," and they wondered how he could live at all when he took so little nourishment. They could explain his having lasted so long only on the ground that he had been miraculously sustained by the Holy Eucharist.

He was frequently ill — sometimes so ill that he was supposed to be dying. He hinted at the cause of this by telling of a Franciscan he had known at the Ara Coeli, a Brother Antonio, who, though he did not macerate his body to any great extent, was always exclaiming, *"Amore langueo, amore langueo!"* and slowly wasted away and died. Time after time Philip's doctors had given him up, but every time he had recovered so suddenly that it seemed a miracle. Yet each time he had assured people that he was not going to die just then, as he still had to reform his life and prepare for death.

He was now obliged to give up some of his activities. At San Giovanni, and for a while at the Vallicella, he had been the confessor for all the members of the community, all of whom usually went to him every day. In 1590 he resigned the office on account of his increasing infirmities. Not since 1576 had he formally preached, though he had sometimes asked questions or made comments. These always thrilled the audience, but he did this seldom because even that much was likely to get him overwhelmed with emotion. After 1589, when he had to stop, choking with tears, he kept an absolute silence. He had a horror of "scenes." But if he was asked why he no longer preached, he would say that he had no talent. "Oh, but you used to preach, Father," the objection would come. "I know," he would return, "but that was only because in the beginning we had so few men available. At that time God supplied the ability I lacked."

He still heard confessions in the church, however, preferring now to hear them there than in his room because in the church he could avoid the conversations that so tired

him. All the same, he had many visitors, though these were
now limited to his intimates. With them he liked to talk
about general literature, and the Oratory was the main center of Platonism in a Rome dominated by Aristotelianism.
Generally the conversation came to spiritual subjects at the
end, even when it did not start there. For the cardinals at
his feet — especially the young Cusano and Federigo Borromeo and that former inmate of the Oratory, the clever
hunchback, Ottavio Paravicini — he conducted what was almost a revival of the Oratory in its primitive form, when he
had gathered his first handful of obscure disciples in his
little room at San Girolamo. Of these the Cardinal Federigo
was a special favorite of his, both on his own account and
because he was a cousin of St. Charles. It was mainly because of Philip's urging that he consented to accept the
archbishopric of Milan.

A much less admirable product of the Oratory was Paolo
Camillo Sfondrato, who, like Paravicini, had been brought
up there as a boy, and who, when his uncle, Gregory XIV,
was elected pope, was immediately created a cardinal. The
nephew took every possible advantage of his position, especially when he came to see that his uncle would not last
long. Bordet remarks: "It was hard to recognise the disciple
of St. Philip under his somewhat vulgar greed." Pastor is
equally scathing.

The Fathers at the Vallicella, however, would have been
more than human had they not flattered themselves that,
through the young cardinal-nephew, their former pupil, and
a pope who for thirty years had been Philip's penitent, the
Oratory might expect many favors. But Philip would ask
for none, and those he obtained came at the Pope's own
instance. It was from Gregory that he received the privilege
of saying Mass in a private chapel and in his own way; and

it was Gregory who gave him permission to say the rosary instead of his office. Of this latter privilege he never availed himself. Even when he was ill he would have one of the Fathers read the Breviary aloud while he followed in silence and rapt attention. If the smallest mistake were made, Philip would be prompt with his correction.

The Pope also told him that he should not hear confessions in church any more, as this drained his energy too much. Philip took this as a piece of advice rather than a positive order, so he did not always do what he had been told. Whenever he felt strong enough he would creep down to his box to perform the spiritual work he most loved, insisting that it was a recreation to him rather than a labor. And indeed there were days and even hours on end when he seemed to be as vigorous as he ever had been.

Philip's relations with Gregory XIV and Clement VIII were more intimate than with any other of the eleven popes who had reigned since his arrival at Rome sixty years earlier, more intimate even than they had been with Gregory XIII. These two men were not only his close friends but had been among his disciples.

He had foretold Gregory's election, when he was Cardinal Sfondrato. For one day when he heard that the Florentine cardinal had called to see him, instead of allowing the Most Illustrious to come upstairs, he went down to the guest room to meet him. There Philip ordered the rest of the people present to kiss the foot of the cardinal, which all of them did, though probably everybody took this as one of Philip's pranks. Whenever Sfondrato called again, Philip would say lightly, "Oh, that pope, eh?" The prediction seemed to be utterly falsified when Urban VII was elected after the death of Sixtus V. But Urban had a reign of only thirteen days. Then Cardinal Sfondrato succeeded him and

Philip's prophecy was fulfilled. His election came at the end of a conclave that lasted nearly two months. If he owed it in part to the King of Spain, he owed it still more to the fact that he had never lifted a finger to obtain the tiara for himself. The Sacred College by that time was glad to fall back upon one who had shown himself so disinterested.

Because of his former close association with the Oratory it is perhaps hardly surprising that the first time Philip called upon him as Pope, he rose and went forward to greet his visitor, and threw his arms about him. Then he did something very much in Philip's own manner. Taking the red biretta he had worn as a cardinal, he put it on Philip's head, saying, "We create you cardinal." Philip with great presence of mind saved himself by treating this as a joke. He whispered something in the Pope's ear and the dignity was for the moment averted. Nevertheless the red biretta was sent to the Vallicella the following day, and Philip had to think quickly again. He returned a message thanking the Pope but saying that he would let him know when he was ready to become a cardinal. Gregory might have insisted had he not known that for Philip it could be no more than a dignity, which would only distress him, and that no active service could be performed by a man so old and ill. Not until the danger had been averted did Philip feel free to jest about it. Then he often asked Monsignor Vestri, the official in charge of such matters, when his cardinalatial brief was going to be prepared. Not every Pope could have been handled in this fashion. But Philip understood Gregory's complaisant disposition. It was the main fault of an otherwise admirable pontiff.

Philip had avoided the dignity for himself; he had trouble again in avoiding it when Gregory, after a short reign, was succeeded by Clement VIII. Here was a man not easily to be put off. Bordini was made a bishop, not greatly to his own sorrow, or perhaps even to Philip's; he had been a somewhat troublesome subject. But Philip saw worse looming ahead. After this everybody who entered his room had his eye caught by two large cardinalatial coats-of-arms hanging there. No explanation was ever given as to what they meant, or why instead of the ordinary bearings, skulls had been drawn. But Philip knew well enough what he meant by the strange emblems; so did others when, shortly after Philip's death, Clement made Baronius and Tarugi cardinals.[1]

Clement was a great pope, a man whose fine build and majestic bearing impressed everybody who came into contact with him. Yet he was mild and courteous and, it was noted, specially gentle with children. Every day he had a number of poor men dine with him, and he sometimes waited on them himself. So much was he a reformer in the Philippine style — in contrast with the stern Pius V and Sixtus V — that Pastor is able to quote the saying current at the time that in him Philip had ascended the throne of the Fisherman. His chief defects were nepotism and a habit of procrastination.

With Clement VIII Philip's relations were no less cordial than they had been with Gregory XIV, and they lasted until Philip's death. Like Gregory, Clement treated Philip as though he were a cardinal, making him sit in his presence with his head covered. Like Gregory XIV, too, and the Gregory before him, he would even kiss Philip's hand as a mark of veneration. They were all quite sure that he was a saint. Those who saw how the Pope treated him, and how

---

[1] It is possible that Clement had spoken to Philip of his intentions and had laid them aside so as not to distress one so near the grave. It is also possible that Philip foresaw by some other illumination what was to come.

completely Philip was at ease with the Pope, used to tell him, "Well, you won't be able to escape this time!" On such occasions Philip would raise his eyes to heaven and exclaim, "Paradise! Paradise!" while tossing his black biretta in the air. Or else he would play football with the red biretta Gregory XIV had sent him a year or two before.

The affectionate familiarity that existed between the two men perhaps comes out most clearly in a letter Philip wrote to Clement towards the end of 1593. It had been preceded by one which must have been in much the same jocular vein, but of which only the gist has been preserved. The occasion was that Philip had been disregarding Gregory's instructions that he had better not wear himself out by hearing confessions in the church. In his first letter Philip made a pretence of being astonished that anyone had supposed that he wished to deprive Clement of the papacy; all the same he asked to be allowed to do as he wished and go, to the church to hear the confessions of three or four poor women. As for cardinals, *their* confessions, of course, he could hear, if necessary, lying in bed! This was followed by a letter, the original of which may still be seen in the sacristy of the Chiesa Nuova. It runs: "Beatissimo Padre: And who am I that cardinals should stoop to come to see me, especially last evening the Cardinal of Florence and Cusano? . . . and that self-same day he tarried with me two full hours after nightfall, and said much good of your Holiness — more, it seems to me, than he ought to have said, because you who are Pope ought to be humility itself. At seven hours after nightfall Jesus came to give Himself to me and to abide with me, and your Holiness takes care not once to come into our church. Jesus Christ is Man and God, and He comes to visit me every time I will; and your Holiness is a simple man, born of the Lady Agnesina, a most holy woman doubtless, while He was born of the Virgin of all virgins. I should have much to say were I to give way to the anger I feel. I command your Holiness to do my bidding in the matter of the girl I wish to put in the Tor di Specchi; she is the daughter of Claudio Neri,[2] whose children your Holiness has promised to care for, and I must remind you that it becomes a Pope to keep his promise. Wherefore let your Holiness put this matter into my hands, so that I may use your name in case of need; the rather that I know the mind of this girl, and am sure she is moved by an inspiration of God. With all befitting humility I kiss the feet of your Holiness."

The Pope was entertained by this letter and wrote under it on the same paper and in his own hand, though in the third person: "The Pope says that the first part of this petition breathes somewhat of an ambitious spirit, in that you tell him that cardinals visit you so often; unless, indeed, you wish to let him know that these are spiritual men, which he knows very well already. As to his not going to see you, he says that your Reverence does not deserve it, since you will not accept the cardinalate so many times offered you. In regard to the *command*, he allows you to scold those good Mothers with your wonted severity if they will not do what you wish; and in his turn he commands you to take care of yourself and not to go back to the confessional without his leave; and that when next our Lord comes to see you, you pray for him and the pressing needs of Christendom."

The "pressing needs of Christendom" was probably a reference to the spiritual rehabilitation of Henry IV, a matter just then being closely considered. But Clement does not

---

[2] He does not seem to have been a relative.

seem to have done anything about the Tor di Specchi, that
rather aristocratic community of Benedictine Oblates into
which it was not very easy to obtain admission. Claudio
Neri's daughter was provided for there not by the Pope but
by Cardinal Alessandrino. Clement was, in fact, inclined to
be niggardly and was always inordinately slow to act about
anything.

Moreover, friendly as he was to Philip and the Congregation of the Oratory, he refused to intervene when Raffaelo
Tarugi, a near relative of the man he was about to create
an archbishop and later a cardinal, was sentenced to death.
He was convicted of being implicated in the depredations of
bandits — as was the case with many men of good family
in those days. The Pope decided that the man deserved his
punishment and that an example should be made, and he
may have felt that to allow personal considerations to affect
the case would damage the administration of justice. Raffaelo was beheaded on June 21, 1592; at the end of the
same year Francesco Maria was made archbishop of
Avignon.

Yet the intimate relations between the Pope and Philip
continued to the end. Shortly before his own death Philip
went to see Clement and found him in bed with gout. "Don't
come near me!" the Pope cried to Philip, afraid that he
would go up to him in his usual affectionate way. "I cannot
bear it if anyone so much as touches the bed." But Philip
told him not to be afraid. "Let me do as I please," he said,
with which he took the Pope's hand and held it to his own
palpitating heart. Immediately the pain was gone, and
Clement regarded what had happened as one more of
Philip's miracles.

Concerning these miracles a word should be said. A great
many of them are recorded — testified to under oath, it must

be remembered — during the Process for Philip's beatification. Though all that evidence is not of equal weight, and though many of the miracles may be explained on other than supernatural grounds, they are certainly not all to be accounted for in this way. Yet often the power of suggestion may possibly be seen operating. Philip told Anna Morona to repeat after him: "Lord, Philip has bid me say in Thy name that he does not wish me to die yet." And she got well. He treated Maria Felice da Castro, a sister at the Tor di Specchi, in much the same way. She was told to say, "Fever, I command thee to depart and leave this creature of Almighty God." Baronius was given the same command when he was suffering from fever. To Antonina Raidi Philip said, "Antonina, take care that you never get ill unless I give you leave." After that, whenever she felt not very well, she would go to him and ask, "Father, do you wish me to be ill?" Nothing pleased him more than such simplicity.

Sometimes, too, the miracles seem to have been an exercise of common-sense rather than of any supernatural power. He found Bradamante Pacelli trying to cure her headache by wrapping bandages around her head. He pulled them off at once — and her headache went. In some instances when he was appealed to, he sent those who wished to be cured a mysterious object which they took to contain relics but which, when examined after his death, turned out to be nothing but part of a vestment used at Mass and an ordinary medal, such as might hang on a child's neck. Received with faith, this served just as well as the laying on of his hands. That he used this method may have been due to the fact that he was often called to go to women in difficult confinements. This was a little embarrassing to him, and he knew that in the majority of cases the course of nature would suffice. When Philip told a sick person, "Don't worry;

it's nothing: you're going to get well," he need not be supposed to have always had a revelation about this from God. Such words, coming from him, can be readily imagined as having more effect upon the mind of the patient than would a similar encouraging remark made by you or me.

Philip had a way of dismissing his miracles lightly. "What's all this talk about miracles?" he used to say. "How should a sinner like myself perform miracles?" And to Baronius he confided: "Cesare, I assure you that it is a great subject of regret to me that people take me for what they do; I constantly pray to God not to do anything through my instrumentality, which may give them occasion to esteem me for what I really am not; and believe me, if at times anything has happened of a supernatural character, it has been through the faith of others, and not through my merits." But when all reasonable reservations have been made, how is one to explain away the following incident?

It occurred in 1592 at a time when Philip was thought to be dying, and the priests who were in his room with the doctors had drawn the curtains round his bed. Suddenly they all heard the voice of the dying man saying very loudly: "Oh, my most holy Madonna! my beautiful Madonna! My blessed Madonna!" The doctors present ran to him, as the bed and the whole room were shaking, and drew back the curtains. There was Philip kneeling, his hands uplifted — and suspended in air. He seemed to be embracing someone whom nobody else could see, and he kept repeating, weeping as he spoke: "No, I am not worthy! Who am I, O my dear Madonna, that you should come to see me? O Virgin most beautiful and most pure, I do not deserve a grace so great! Why have you come to me, the least and lowest of your servants? Who am I? O holiest Virgin! O Mother of God! O blessed amongst women!"

The doctors spoke to him and asked him what was the matter, and he answered, "Did you not see the Mother of God come to visit me and to take away my pain?" Then, realising where he was, he immediately sank down on the bed, drew the covers over his head, and burst into floods of tears. Have it, if you will, that Philip was delirious. Does that account for his body lifted into the air? Yet levitation is something that was seen to happen to him over and over again. And what except a miracle can account for his instantaneous cure. "I do not need you now," he told the doctors, smiling; "the most holy Madonna has made me well." About that there was no doubt; one of the doctors felt his pulse: it showed that Philip was perfectly cured.

We know the names of the doctors present. One of them, Angelo Vettori da Bagnorea, wrote out an account of the occurrence before any of the details could slip his mind. Even if it be suggested that Philip had healed himself by his powers of suggestion, that does not get around the fact that his body hung there only a yard or so away from several people who were in the room with him. Is the state of anybody's mind enough to suspend the laws of gravitation? And so with many other miraculous happenings we hear of in Philip's life. They may not all have been miracles in the strict sense. And it is possible that some of the witnesses to them may have been a little uncritical. But at least some of the miracles must be accepted if the ordinary rules of evidence are followed. All the three hundred witnesses at Philip's Process cannot have been either fools or liars. The weight of their testimony can be rejected only if we close our minds and set up an iron dogma that declares that miracles cannot possibly happen.

During these last three years of his life — especially then — Philip lived in almost unbroken prayer. He was often lost in ecstasy, still more often in a reverie which came close to being the same thing. Gallonio says that many times he entered Philip's room while he was dressing and found him completely lost to what he was supposed to be doing and standing in the middle of the floor with his eyes fixed on heaven and holding a garment in his hand. Gallonio was reminded at such times of the pictures he had seen of St. Martin of Tours dividing his cloak.

Philip had now withdrawn from all responsibility in order to give himself wholly to the contemplative life — the life for which he had always secretly hungered. For this reason he obtained the Pope's permission to resign the office of Provost and then assembled the Fathers to announce his decision. The house at Naples having reluctantly concurred that he should be released from his burden, Baronius, with equal reluctance, accepted the office to which he was now elected. When the community went up one by one as the rule prescribed to kiss the hand of the new superior, Baronius sent them first to kiss the hand of Philip. He was no longer the head of the Oratory; he would always be its soul.

About him he gathered a group of very young men who looked after him and upon whom he showered his love. One of these was Pietro Consolini. To him Philip said at their first meeting, when Pietro was a student at Rome, "Courage, my son; you are one of us." A little later, without saying anything to Pietro about what was in his mind, his intuition led him to do something quite without precedent at the Oratory or in any religious order: he proposed his name as a novice and got him accepted. Now it was to Pietro that the aged Philip made confidences made to nobody else. It was with Pietro that Philip usually said his office. It was on Pietro's arm that Philip always leaned. Gallonio meanwhile lived at call in the room just underneath Philip's. These two young men, along with Germanico Fedeli, were in a special way attached to him and were at his personal service.

Philip also had some young men outside the Oratory who served in a somewhat similar way. One was Francesco Zazzara, son of that Monte Zazzara the perfumer who was one of Philip's first disciples. Francesco was a law-student and it was his function to sweep out the room while Philip was saying Mass. He was also employed in such little odd jobs as arranging Philip's cupboards or distributing Philip's alms or making rosaries for Philip. He was almost too closely attached, for Philip had to send him away when he wanted to pray. Merely to look at the old saint was for Francesco a happiness. "When the Father was ill," he related afterwards, "I used to stand there for two or three hours, with my hat in my hand, without his seeing me, and this I did because it seemed to me that I was looking at a saint, and such was my devotion to him that I never tired of looking at him." From him come many of the details about Philip's declining years.

Ottavio Paravicini, another of his close friends, was at this time not precisely a young man, for he was getting on to forty; but he was, of course, still a boy to one who had had charge of his education from the time he was six until he was twenty-seven. He had been made a cardinal by Gregory XIV in 1591, but he still delighted to wait on Philip, making his bed and sweeping his room out for him. One day when Philip was ill he sent everybody except the Cardinal out of the room and then said to him, "Ottavio, I want to speak a little to you, but if my cough obliges me to spit, I wonder if you would mind handing me the basin, as you used to do before you were a cardinal." And the Most Illustrious little hunchback answered, "Father, this is the greatest kindness you could do me. I feel myself unworthy of such an honor."

Older cardinals had, as was to be expected, a somewhat different mode of expressing their admiration. Capecelatro, who was himself to become a cardinal, dwells in his magnificent life of Philip with a kind of naïve satisfaction upon the number of dignitaries who frequented Philip's room. But for that matter, most of the members of the Sacred College went to see Philip at one time or another during his last years, and several of them were his intimates or his penitents. Two of them gave him striking tributes by writing books about him while he was still alive.

One was by the humanist Gabriel Paleotto, of whom it is reported that he never allowed a day to pass on which he did not read some Greek, and who is described by the Abbé Bordet as "a good Christian and an honest man." When a few months after Philip's death the Cardinal's *De Bono Senectutis* appeared, it had a portrait of Philip as a frontispiece, for the book held up Philip as the most charming of models for old age.

The dialogue of Cardinal Valiero, *Philip or Christian Cheerfulness*, was as befitted the work of another humanist, also in Latin. The main force of the Renaissance had spent itself, but Valiero belonged enough to that time to avoid being too crudely Christian in his forms of expression and tried to give a classical elegance to his production by calling Philip the "Christian Socrates." "Assuredly," he wrote, "may that great man be styled a Christian Socrates who despises all outward things, and who is the mightiest and most dreaded enemy of every vice, who follows after virtue, who is the master and teacher of sincerity and a blameless life, who is in all his doings an example of charity; a man who

gives himself in lavish charity to all, who compassionates
the weakness of all, who aids all with his instructions and
counsels, and commends all to the most high God with holy
prayers, and who amidst so many cares preserves a constant
and unclouded cheerfulness." The description beguiles but
is perhaps a little too much in the humanist convention fully
to convey a sense of Philip's sanctity.

Philip himself, we may surmise, would have felt more
honored had Valiero, instead of comparing him to Socrates,
compared him to his unlettered friend Felice da Cantalice,
the Capuchin lay-brother who died in 1587. Far more than
learning he valued simplicity. That Fra Felice was so completely devoid of worldly wisdom as even to be unaware
that such a thing existed always charmed Philip. Once he
knelt for the lay-brother's blessing; another time when Felice
asked for the blessing, Philip knelt and demanded it too.
That time they knelt with their arms around one another
in a contest of humility which reminds one of the meeting
between King Louis of France and Brother Giles, when they
parted as friends without either having spoken a word.

But cheerful though Philip was even in illness, he was
now feeling his infirmities a good deal. Until towards the
end the heat of his body had been so intense that he used
to go out with his cassock unbuttoned and laughing at the
young men shivering in their wraps. When the order came
in Gregory XIII's time that all priests were to wear a cotta
in the confessional, Philip presented himself before the Pope
with his cassock unbuttoned as usual, and Gregory asked
him why. Philip explained and said, "Yet you want me to
wear a cotta as well!" "Oh no," the Pope answered; "we do
not mean the order to apply to you; you do as you like."

It was an ominous sign when a man who, until then, had
had something cooling mixed with all his medicines, began

to feel the cold. The fire of devotion was still in his breast, but there was so little left of that wasted body to contain it. He huddled up to the hearth in his room and rarely left the house. The letters of those who lived with him indicate that they were very uneasy on this account. Yet Philip was still sure that he was not going to die when they thought he was dying. Over and over again he had made his sudden recoveries and had told the astonished doctors that it was all due to the prayers offered for him. He constantly said that spiritual persons always received an intimation of their death; he had had no such intimation as yet.

As characteristic of him as his joy — even more character- istic — was his humility. "If I get well," he told one of his visitors, "I intend to change my life." To Federigo Borromeo he said that it was not for him to desire death like St. Paul, because he first wished to do a little good, something he had never done. "Ah, poor me," he used to exclaim, "how many ignorant peasants, how many poor girls will be far above me in paradise!" With the Consecrated Host in his hand at Mass, he protested every day to Christ, "Lord, be- ware of me today, lest I should betray Thee!" One of his favorite maxims was, "Let me get through today, and I shall not fear for tomorrow."

Perhaps it was because of his joy and humility and sim- plicity that this great mystic never experienced anything even remotely resembling the long stretches of aridity of which we almost invariably hear in the lives of contem- platives. Or perhaps it was a special grace. One is left, how- ever, with a feeling that this was due, at least in part, to his natural disposition; his fervent joy never left him because he was utterly devoid of any tendency toward introspection.

He not only had no spiritual system but we do not hear of him studying the systems that had been so elaborately worked out during his own lifetime by St. Teresa and St. John of the Cross, among others. Yet he left his own imprint upon the new school of mysticism that was about to arise. The young Francis de Sales, still a layman, was in Rome in 1591. Whether or not he became intimately acquainted with Philip is doubtful; but there is no doubt at all that he became deeply impregnated with Philip's spirit, which he passed on, blended with moderating Teresian mysticism, to St. Vincent de Paul and St. Jane Frances de Chantal. In fact, he passed on to the whole world what he had heard and seen in Rome — an easy familiarity with God which made the technique of mysticism almost a domestic utensil. So for Philip, he taught his disciples to address our Lady not as the Queen of Heaven or even the Mother of God but with the endearing diminutive of *Mamma*. Yet he taught more by his personality than by anything that he said that there is a short cut to union with God — short enough to the simple and humble.

It is no wonder that his was a life of radiant happiness. A beautiful instance of this was when his beloved Nicolò Gigli died in 1591. Philip was so sure that he had gone to heaven that, instead of shedding any tears, he waited until he thought the church was empty. Then he was seen by somebody, who secretly watched, to be bending over Gigli's body, covering it with kisses and laughing in exultation.

Since his illness of 1562 Philip had never really been well. Perhaps this was true of him ever since he had had his experience in the catacomb of San Sebastiano just before Whitsunday of 1544. For it was then that the extraordinary palpitations began which so exhausted him and which, though they gave him such a sense of sweetness, were also, as he confessed to Consolini and Cardinal Federigo Borromeo, the true cause of his periods of sickness. Like his friend the Franciscan who was always murmuring *Amore langueo*, he was languishing away, lovesick for God. For whole days he would be prostrate with this sublime affliction. Many nights no sleep would come to him for the same reason. Then his disciples would try to give him some rest by refusing to bring him Holy Communion when he lay ill in bed. "No, no," he would cry, "give me my Lord, and then I will go to sleep at once!" It was like a child promising to be good. And once when Gallonio seemed to him to delay a little in putting the Host on his tongue, he exclaimed, "Antonio, why do you not give me my Lord at once!"

To quiet his palpitations he had had himself often bled, and he continued to do so, though now there was little enough blood in his veins. Once he even attempted to bleed himself, and brought on a hemorrhage. That was in 1587, and he did not doctor himself again. But he insisted on having this remedy applied to him only twelve days before his death. While always obeying his doctors, he used to tell them that he had slight faith in their ministrations. On one occasion after he had collapsed and they had brought him to by putting hot iron against his skin, he smiled up at them and said that there was nothing the matter with him except what they had done to him.

Medical science at that time, of course, left much to be desired; yet the best modern doctors might have been at a loss as to how to treat him. All of a sudden he would fall ill, for no apparent cause, and get well as suddenly. Even during his last days he made what appeared to be an unaccountable recovery. Then the octogenarian bounded like a boy up to his *loggia*. The doctors remarked that they had not seen him looking so well in ten years. When they had gone he turned to the Fathers in his room and said, "They think I am cured, but I am still very ill." It was different from that time in 1592 when he had been supposed to be dying. Then he had told his penitents not to choose a permanent spiritual director as he would be up before Christmas to hear their confessions again.

He had been right then, and he was right now. On May 13, 1595, he joked with the doctors, telling them, "Be off with you; my remedies are a great deal better than yours. This morning very early I sent alms to several convents to have Masses and prayers said for me, and I have not spit any blood since then and I am quite free from pain. Look at me; am I not in perfect health?" But when Germanico Fedeli had to leave on the eighteenth to go a day's journey from Rome, Philip warned him to be sure to be back by the eve of Corpus Christi. Four days before that feast he said to his friend Nero del Nero, "I am quite cured and feel at this moment that nothing is the matter with me; but be sure of this — I have only a few days to live." Two days later when Consolini told him that there was no need to say a Mass for a man who had completely recovered, Philip returned, "Say a Mass for the Dead for me; I know how I am."

Corpus Christi fell in 1595 on May 25. That day Philip said Mass for the last time in his little chapel, but a good deal earlier than usual. He did not say it in private this time; it was attended by several friends, to whom he gave Holy Communion. They noticed that before he began he looked out for a while over the Janiculum hill and Sant' Onofrio. It seemed a strange proceeding; they understood afterwards that he was taking his farewell of a spot dear to him. They noticed also that when Philip came to the *Gloria* he sang the words, though it was a low Mass.

All that day he sat in his room hearing confessions and receiving visitors. At evening Cardinal Cusano came and

Philip sat with him talking and then heard his confession. When they parted, Philip went with him to the head of the stairs and gazed earnestly a long while into his face. He said nothing, but he knew that they were parting for the last time. On the twelfth Cardinal Federigo had given him the Viaticum. On the twenty-fifth Philip, on saying farewell, kissed him on the tonsure. It was due to Philip's urging that the Cardinal had just consented to accept the Archbishopric of Milan.

When the last visitor had departed Philip ate two eggs for his supper and got into bed. Nobody was worrying about him, for he had seemed his old self all that day. Yet two days before he had destroyed all his papers, and that night when some of the Fathers came to say goodnight and ask his blessing they heard him murmuring words to which they attached no importance then but whose meaning they grasped later. Like a child playing a game or memorizing a lesson he sing-songed, "Two and three are five, three and three are six." He was foretelling the hour of his death — the sixth hour or, as we reckon time, two in the morning.

At that hour Gallonio, who slept in the room immediately below his and who was all ready for a summons, heard Philip moving about. Running upstairs, he found him choking with blood and phlegm. He at once sent for the doctors. By the time they arrived Philip had managed to get rid of the congestion and again appeared to be all right. But he told them, "There is nothing you can do; I am dying."

The community were summoned and crowded into the room where they saw Philip sitting on the bed like one half asleep. It was Baronius who cried, "Father, are you leaving us without a word? Give us at least your blessing." At this Philip opened his eyes, raised them towards heaven; then with a faint smile he made a movement with his hand as though trying to give them the blessing they asked. Immediately afterwards he drew a long sigh and, still sitting on the bed, quietly died. The hour of his death was the same as the hour of his birth. He was within two months of eighty.

Chapter Fourteen

FOUR SPANIARDS AND A SAINT

WITNESSES at the Process of Philip's Beatification testified that at the hour of his death they had seen him — some of them in dream, others in vision. The majority of these people were nuns. The most impressive case was that of Caterina Paluzzi, who was a Dominican tertiary in a convent some distance from Rome and who did not hear of his death until a few days after it occurred. To her an old man appeared in priest's vestments and resplendent in glory. When she told her confessor about the vision he asked her to describe the features of the man she had seen. Then he showed her a picture of Philip, and she exclaimed, "Why, that is the old man I saw!"

Things of this sort were related with edification, but may possibly be explained on other than supernatural grounds. So, for that matter, may be the famous meeting by bilocation which is supposed to have occurred during Philip's lifetime between himself and St. Catherine de' Ricci. About this the accounts are a little vague. It was taken as a proof of his having seen Catherine that he said, on being shown her portrait, that it was not very like her, for her face was more joyous. He could have heard a good deal about her from Animuccia who twice went to see her; and her uncle, Fra Diaceto, who was prior at the Minerva during the reign of Paul IV and a friend of Philip's, could have supplied further information. Nor is it impossible that Philip had seen her when she was a child in Florence. If there actually was bilocation, it would seem to have been on Catherine's part.

These things are related here, not because they are necessarily true, but because they indicate the mood of many people immediately following Philip's death. He himself had very little trust in such manifestations. As the Abbé Bordet points out: "Spiritual guides admit the possibility of illusions and give strict rules for discovering them, but Philip surpasses them all in severity. . . . It may be said that in his opinion illusions were the rule, and true spiritual experiences a rare exception." And illusions apart, there are such things as telepathy and second sight.

So also with regard to Philip's prophecies. Some of them are indeed very remarkable. Others may not be prophecies at all, in the sense of implying supernatural illumination. "What would you do," Philip asked Francesco della Molara, "if your wife were to die?" When she did die soon afterwards that was regarded as a prophecy. Other things of the same sort, though more definite, may have been merely lucky shots. Except for predictions that he explicitly said were made by inspiration, we may take most of them as remarks tossed over his shoulder, the kind of predictions we all make, though without Philip's high average of accuracy. One often feels that people read into his words more than he ever intended. At the same time one cannot avoid the conclusion, from the evidence presented, that his life was full of marvels, the chief marvel being his life itself.

His miracles were so numerous that Bacci had to classify them, with a chapter on each variety. The most famous of all these miracles, however, leaves an element of doubt in the mind. It was that of Philip's raising the dead son of his friend Fabrizio de' Massimi to life. Yet the truthfulness of the witnesses is beyond doubt, as should be the inherent possibility of the occurrence. As St. Paul said before Agrippa: "Why should it be thought an incredible thing with you, that God should raise the dead?" The really incredible thing is that anybody should profess belief in God and deny the miraculous. Such an affirmation coupled with such a denial involves a grotesque contradiction in terms. Whatever doubts arise about this particular miracle are on account of the circumstances surrounding it.

The facts themselves are given very explicitly and were sworn to on oath by the father, the boy's step-mother, and a servant, all of whom were present. It was on March 16, 1583, that Paolo de' Massimi died, after having received the Last Sacraments from the parish priest. When Philip arrived he called the boy, "Paolo! Paolo!" and Paolo opened his eyes. There was a conversation lasting about a quarter of an hour, during which Philip asked Paolo if he would not like to die and go to see his mother and sister in heaven. Paolo said he would, and then died again. The question inevitably arises whether he was really dead when Philip got to the house. For what was the point of bringing him to life for so short a period? Here the testimony is unsatisfactory. His aunt suggested to the Auditors of the Rota that the boy "perhaps had something to confess." But she was not there, and those who were there say nothing about any confession made to Philip. All that one can conclude is that the eye-witnesses *believed* that Paolo had been brought back from the dead.

Rome was full of people who were equally certain that Philip performed miracles. But they apparently did not speak much about this while he was alive, and the writer of the anonymous life in manuscript at the Vallicella remarks that Philip "hid the gifts of God with so much care that we, who were constantly with him for so many years, even we could know but little about them." In other words, the Fathers of the Congregation were surprised by hearing some of the evidence that was given at the Process.

Yet in face of the evidence, it is impossible to doubt that the miraculous did frequently occur, or not to wonder at the frame of mind which would rule such evidence out of court. What may, however, be reasonably suggested is that among people who were deeply stirred by the discovery that they had had a saint living among them for sixty years, there may have sometimes been an enthusiastic tendency to see something marvellous in everything that Philip had done or said — when it was looked at in retrospect. But when all the discounts have been made, the fact remains that the witnesses were people who knew Philip — as all Rome knew him; that they gave their evidence in the place where the happenings had occurred and where it could be checked; and that it was carefully weighed by men whose profession it was to examine such matters. Subtractions may be legitimate; a total subtraction is not. The Abbé Ponnelle cautiously sums up with: "We can inquire more critically than Philip's contemporaries before we admit the genuineness of all the miracles held up to our admiration. A large number of the events which they accepted as such seem to us very insignificant, though it is true to say that, even though they may not show any supernatural influence, they give us a very vivid picture of Philip's methods. Even though they may not always reveal the wonder-worker, they often add picturesque detail to the portrait of the saint." With which opinion we may let the matter rest.

Philip's was perhaps the last instance of what amounted to canonization by acclaim, in the old style. The strict formal process was adhered to and was begun just two months after his death, on August 2, 1595. It went on until June 1, 1601, when it was interrupted. But between February 12, 1605, and February 21 of the same year it was completed. And during these two periods over three hundred people gave evidence, some trivial enough but some of it very important.[1] Yet the more interesting and striking fact is that a kind of informal process of canonization began from the day of Philip's death. It might also be pointed out that miracles took place even before his body was buried and that they multiplied when he was in his tomb.

So sure was everybody that Philip was a great saint that there was official connivance at proceedings which would usually have been severely reprehended. The publication of his portrait, aureoled and with the title of Blessed printed beneath it, was allowed. In 1596 the Abbate Maffa hung a lamp where Philip was buried in the Vallicella, and there it burned day and night. Though this lamp was taken away by the Filippini, who feared that they might damage Philip's cause by an unauthorized cultus, Clement gave permission that it might be put back, whereupon Costanza del Dragho hung a still more splendid lamp there. Already many "ex votos" were arriving. The Pope himself said very solemnly, "We hold him to be a saint."

Baronius, as Provost, without in the least questioning this belief, nevertheless considered that it was proper to have prayers offered for Philip, as for any other departed soul. Marcello Vitelleschi, a Canon of St. Peter's, on the other hand, could not bring himself to say the *De Profundis* but said instead the *Laudate Dominum omnes gentes* customary at the death of infants. And Girolamo Beger, the Dominican, whose vocation to religion had been foretold so many

---

[1] And not all of these, of course, had anything miraculous to relate. Much of the evidence bore simply on Philip's heroic virtue.

years before by Philip, declared when preaching at the Minerva that there was no need to pray for one who most assuredly was already in heaven. When the first anniversary of the death came round even Baronius substituted for the usual requiem a festival as for a saint. Cardinals attended subsequent celebrations, and in the 1597 edition of the Martyrology Philip's name was included among that of the *Beati*. In 1598 the room Philip had occupied was made into a chapel, in which they placed the altar at which he used to say Mass, hanging above it his portrait as of a saint. And when on May 24, 1602, Philip's body was translated to a new resting-place, Mass was said at his tomb, though that time the Pope thought that the Fathers had gone too far. That all this was permitted is a clear indication that the Process was looked upon as a mere matter of form and that everybody, from the Pope down, regarded Philip's canonization assured. He was in effect canonized many years before the official decision was handed down.

This sort of thing would not have been possible under Urban VIII, for he issued an exceedingly strict decree against anticipating the declarations of the Holy See regarding sanctity. But Urban did not ascend the papal throne until 1623, and though the rules he promulgated were supposed to be, in a general way, already in force, this was regarded as an occasion when ordinary rules did not apply. Even during Philip's lifetime there had been enthusiasts who used to pray, "*Sancte Philippe, ora pro nobis.*" And though that is not to be defended, other instances of excessive devotion may perhaps be covered by Capecelatro's comment that they "may be lightly deemed mere fond exaggerations of piety; but true piety is love, and all real love, be it human or divine, is outside of conventional rules, and to those who do not love, its expressions appear excessive and even meaningless."

Before Philip was buried an autopsy was made on his body. It was then that the doctors found that some of his ribs were broken and pushed outwards, and that his heart was abnormally large, as was the pulmonary artery. There were no other physical peculiarities. Angelo Vettori, one of the doctors, published in 1613 a monograph on the subject. Naturally he is unable to vouch for Philip's own explanation as to how this condition came about. What was the observation of all who knew him was that the hammer strokes of his enlarged heart were in some way connected with his spiritual fervor.

The immediate effect on Philip's death upon the Congregation he had founded was a clearer perception of his ideas and a whole-hearted acceptance of them. During the last days of his life Philip had drawn up, or had dictated, what Baronius called his "last testament" and the "corner stone" of the Oratory. While Philip's body was awaiting burial the decree of May 26 was issued and unanimously adopted by the Fathers. It dealt with the question of vows, on which there had hitherto been some disagreement on the part of those who believed that the Congregation should take them. The words were: "If in the future any member of the Congregation conceives the idea of introducing vows, and speaks of it either in public or private, he and those who follow him are to be considered as excluded and separated from our Congregation by that very fact, and shall thenceforth make no claim to anything whatsoever, any more than if he had never belonged to our Congregation." With this decree was irrevocably affirmed what had always been Philip's concept of the Oratory. The Fathers at Naples could not do other than accept the decision, though some among them had inclined to the view that the Congregation would, and should, develop into a religious order. The point about the vows was made even more emphatic when in 1612 the Constitutions were drawn up and received the approbation of the Holy See.

Two days after his death Philip was laid to rest under the high altar at the Chiesa Nuova. Four years later his body was found incorrupt, as it was again in 1602 and 1639. Since 1922 it has lain in a crystal urn and is now exposed to the veneration of the faithful. The decree of Philip's beatification was pronounced by Paul V on May 25, 1615, and he was canonized on March 12, 1622, by Gregory XV.

If the beatification took as long as it did, this was because Clement VIII, who was always slow to act, felt that he also had to take into account the cause of the founder of the Jesuits. Ignatius had been dead for thirty-nine years in 1595, which was a good reason for the Pope's wish to avoid favoritism in the case of Philip. Moreover the cause of Charles Borromeo — who died in 1584 and was canonized in 1610 — was just then occupying the attention of the Rota. So Philip had to wait.

When he was canonized four other saints were canonized at the same time. They were Ignatius Loyola, Francis Xavier, Isidore the Farmer, and Teresa of Ávila. The current witticism bandied about on March 12, 1622, was that on that day the Pope had canonized "four Spaniards and a saint." There were still many people in Rome who had known Philip, and even those who had never seen him regarded him as their own saint. Spaniards as a race were not very popular among them.

BIBLIOGRAPHICAL NOTE

There is no pretence that this book represents any original research. If it comes to that, there would seem to be little room for anything of the sort after the minute investigations done by Louis Ponnelle and Louis Bordet. Their study — translated into English under the title of St. *Philip Neri and the Roman Society of His Times* (London, 1932) — has been freely used to correct and supplement the earlier biographers. But in these, too, St. Philip Neri has been fortunate. Bacci had few superiors among the hagiographers of the seventeenth century. His *Life of St. Philip Neri* was translated by F. W. Faber and published in two volumes in 1847, and again by F. I. Antrobus in 1902. I have used the one-volume edition of Capecelatro's *St. Philip Neri*, translated by T. A. Pope (London, 1926). Of these authorities, it is perhaps enough to say here that Bacci is closest to his subject, but writes in the manner of his time, a little too much for edification; that Capecelatro, while also somewhat addicted to the giving of edification, has produced a work of art as well as of scholarship; and that Ponnelle and Bordet have gone back to re-examine all the documents again, doing so not only with the most painstaking care but presenting a mass of new findings with literary brilliance.

Hardly less useful to me than these three works has been Ludwig von Pastor's *History of the Popes,* of which Vols. VII to XXIII, translated by Ralph Francis Kerr, all touch St. Philip's period. Of subsidiary importance were the three books by Lady Amabel Kerr: *The Life of Cesare Cardinal Baronius* (London, 1898), *A Precursor of St. Philip, Buonsignore Cacciaguerra* (London, 1903), and *A Son of St. Francis, St. Felix of Cantalice* (London, 1900). Other books useful to me were Cecatelli's *Life of S. Camillus of Lellis,* in two volumes (London, 1851), *Goethe's Travels in Italy,* the English translation of which was published

241

in London in 1885, Evelyn Underhill's *Jacopone da Todi* (London, 1919), and Margaret Yeo's *Reformer: St. Charles Borromeo* (Milwaukee, 1938).

It should be mentioned that there is an excellent short popular life in English available, the *St. Philip Neri* by Father T. V. Matthews of the London Oratory (London, 1934). But it is only about a third of the length of mine. Father Matthews has kindly advised me about the preparation of my book. To the Very Reverend Vincent G. Scharff, Provost of the Oratory at Rock Hill, South Carolina, I am indebted for the reading of my manuscript and for some useful suggestions, and to Mr. Cornelius J. Carr, S.J., of Woodstock College, for the making of the index.

INDEX

Acquaviva, Claudius, S.J., 178, 188
Agnesina, Lady, 217
Agrippa II, King, 235
Aldobrandini, Cardinal Ippolito, *see* Clement VIII, Pope
Aldobrandini, Cardinal Pietro, 106
Alessandrino, Cardinal, 127, *see* Bonelli
Alessi, Tito degli, Barnabite, 128–129, 160
Alexander VI, Pope, 170
Altieri, Lorenzo, 180, 183
Altoviti, Giovanni Battista, 132
Amatis, Fabio de, 89
Ames, Louis, 34, 62, 163–164
Ancina, Giovanni Giovenale, Oratorian, 130, 189, 203, 210
Ancina, Giovanni Mateo, Oratorian, 130
Anerio, Giovanni Francesco, 86, 88
Angelico, Fra, O.P., 6
Animuccia, Giovanni, 8, 86, 87, 89–90, 99, 113, 193, 233
Annals, The, 83, 101–106, 209
Anne of Poland, Queen, 204
Antoninus, St., 6, 9
Antonio, Brother, O.F.M., 212
Antony of Padua, St., 130
Antrobus, F. I., Oratorian, 14 *n.*
Aquinas, St. Thomas, 11, 184
Archconfraternity of Charity, 52–53, 66 *n.*, 68, 71
Aristotelianism, 213
Augustinians, 30, 94, 103

Bacci, Pietro J., 2 *n.; on* beginning

of P.'s work, 32; *on* the building of the Vallicella, 138–139; *on* fervor of Confraternity of Pilgrims and Convalescents, 44; *on* Francesco Pucci of Palestrina, 171; *on* membership of the Congregation, 141; *on* persecution of P., 71; *on* P. as a confessor, 60 *on* P. and music, 91; *on* P.'s attitude toward visions, 187; *on* P.'s charity, 194; *on* P.'s discipline, 137; *on* P.'s jests, 179; *on* P.'s miracles, 234; *on* P.'s mortification, 198; *on* P.'s mystical experiences, 40; *on* P.'s picnics, 95; *on* P.'s powers, 199; *on* P.'s prophetic powers, 142; *on* P.'s retirement for prayer, 16; *on* P.'s resolve, 17; *on* P.'s stay at San Germano, 14 *n.; on* P.'s studies, 29; *on* P.'s temptations, 28 *n.; on* P.'s visits to Monte Cassino and Gaeta, 15; *on* P.'s qualities, 111; *on* seniority at San Girolamo, 54
Balduino, Fra, 7
Barnabites, 30, 128–130, 170
Baronius, Cardinal Cesare, Oratorian, 27, 76, 83–85, 99–107, 114, 115, 118, 131, 146, 148, 170, 207–209, 216, 220, 221, 223, 231, 237, 238, 239
Bathori of Poland, King Stephen, 204
Beger, Girolamo, O.P., 171, 237–238
Bellarmine, St. Robert, 102, 169, 193
Benedict, St., 16

243